VIOLIN OWNER'S MANUAL

SOUVENIR PRESS

Contents by James N. McKean ©2001 James N. McKean
All other contents ©2001 by String Letter Publishing, Inc.
David A. Lusterman, Publisher

First Published in United States of America 2001 by
String Letter Publishing, Inc.

First Published in Great Britain 2002 by
Souvenir Press Ltd.,
43 Great Russell Street, London WC1B 3PD

ISBN: 0 285 63652 9

The right of String Letter Publishing to be identified as author of this work has been asserted by
them in accordance with the Copyright, Designs and Patents Act 1988.

Illustrations: pp. 2, 36, Christie's; pp. 18, 20, 40, Bonhams; pp. 7, 18, 21, 81, 134, Daniel Larson;
pp. 8, 10, 49, Joseph Grubaugh and Signrun Seifert; pp. 42, 117, Skinner; pp. 4, 5, 14, 36, 57, 58,
61, 63, 68, 72, 73, 89, 98, 105, 111, 112, 114, Barbara Gelfand; pp. 16, 23, 25, 77, 78, 108, 110,
125, 126, 130, 132, 135, James N. McKean; pp. 12, 21, 102, 118, Sotheby's; pp.28, 53, Jessamyn
Reeves-Brown; p. 47, William Robert Scott; p. 49, Benjamin Ruth; pp. 36, 68, 89, 98, 105, 111,
112, Trpti Todd; p. 75, Kadenza; p. 83, J. D'Addario and Co.; p. 80, Ithaca, L.R. Baggs, Fishman
Transducers; p. 94, Zeta; p. 101, Phillips; p. 122, Peg Baumgartel

Printed and bound in Great Britain by
The Bath Press, CPI Group, Bath.

VIOLIN OWNER'S MANUAL

THE COMPLETE GUIDE

Know Your Instrument

Protect Your Investment

Sound Your Best

CONTENTS

PRESERVE AND PROTECT YOUR INVESTMENT

UNDERSTAND COMMON REPAIRS

REFERENCE

INTRODUCTION

Whether players or listeners, we all have a love affair with the violin and its sound. The romantic notion of this instrument permeates so many aspects of our history and culture; the violin straddles the worlds of high society and grassroots community with ease and elegance. It transcends the boundaries of classical music and spills into nearly every genre of music making, including jazz, rock 'n' roll, country, folk, blues, and more. Our affection for the violin keeps its sound up-to-date and fresh. And each year manufacturers present new setups, pickups, cases, and strings that produce better sound, better protection, or better performance capabilities.

This manual is designed to provide you with an overview of the many varied and complex aspects of owning and playing a violin in the 21st century. The following pages contain a wealth of information and valuable advice. (If you come across unfamiliar terminology, be sure to turn to our glossary on page 139.) Discover the basics about your violin and bow—including the unreliability of makers' labels. Follow the long path that bow makers have taken to devise contemporary designs, and take a crash course in the role of the bass bar and the soundpost in your instrument. Become a savvy consumer: pick up tips on purchasing the instrument and bow that are right for you, find the instrument case to fit your specific needs, and learn what to do when it's time to sell your current instrument. Some violin repairs and maintenance jobs can be done at home, but most—as you will read—should be entrusted only to a reliable repair shop. Our section on common repairs gives you a better understanding of why procedures are done and whether or not your violin really needs to take a visit to the shop. We hope to save you both time and money with the information and tips gathered in this book.

From humidity control and theft prevention to cleaning and caring for your instrument, the knowledgeable makers and players who have contributed to this text reveal the fundamentals every violin owner should know.

—*Heather K. Scott*

PUBLISHER'S NOTE

This book was compiled by American experts, but where appropriate we have provided additional information regarding British resources. The web sites mentioned are those carrying information of use to British readers. For further listings of resources you will find the *British and International Music Yearbook* (Rhinegold Publishing, London) very useful.

KNOW YOUR INSTRUMENT AND BOW

WHAT IS A VIOLIN?

by Heather K. Scott

There is little question that the violin is the most famous member of the stringed-instrument family—and by far the most distributed musical instrument in the world. Its popularity stems from the sound it produces—a sound hauntingly similar to the human voice. The instrument evolved during the Renaissance from its medieval bowed-instrument predecessors: the lira da braccio and the rebec. Unlike its cousin the viol, the violin has a fretless fingerboard, with strings connected to tuning pegs and a tailpiece (passing over a bridge held taut by the pressure of the strings).

The violin belongs to the family of chordophones, a classification within the Sachs-Hornbostel system, which was devised to categorize instruments that produce sound through the vibration of strings. Chordophones are further divided into four subtypes: lutes, zithers, lyres, and harps (in accordance with how the strings are positioned in relation to the instrument's body). The violin is a member of the subcategory lutes, because of its narrow neck, which protrudes from the resonating body, as well as its strings, which run along the neck to tuning pegs.

Because stringed instruments are made from wood, an easily perishable material, their history before written documentation is largely unknown. Our knowledge of early violins is limited to the ancient cultures of East and South Asia, Mesopotamia, and the Mediterranean. Historians depend solely on iconographic sources as there are no surviving specimens.

The closest relative of the modern violin was born in Italy, and its earliest creators were Gasparo da Salò, Andrea Amati, and Giovanni Paolo Maggini. This trio set proportions used in modern instruments by the end of the 16th century. (Earlier instruments are recognizable by their deeply arched bellies and backs; this group's newer violins were shallower, producing a larger, louder tone.) Makers such as Antonio Stradivari perfected these early designs, shaping the violin into the instrument we know today.

HOW DOES THE VIOLIN PRODUCE SOUND?

The bridge acts as the transmitter that carries the strings' vibrations to the belly of the violin, where the sound-board can be found. The soundboard is supported by a bass bar, a narrow wooden bar that runs lengthwise into the belly. A soundpost (a cylinder usually made from pine) sits inside the instrument, under the treble foot of the bridge and between the belly and the back, and carries the sound further into the instrument's back. This gives the violin its characteristic sound and tone. When the violin's strings are plucked or drawn with a bow, the vibrations travel down this path and reverberate within the instrument, producing the sound you hear. The strength of attack creates a crescendo or decrescendo of sound.

During the 17th century, the violin took over the post the viol had previously held as primary stringed instrument in chamber music. One of the first important violin ensembles was France's Les 24 Violons du Roi (24 Violins for the King), established in 1626. Some of the early composers who began writing for violin virtuosos were Arcangelo Corelli (a virtuoso himself), Antonio Vivaldi, Giuseppe Tartini, and of course J.S. Bach. As the 18th century progressed, major composers such as Mozart, Brahms, Grieg, and Beethoven also began writing solo music for the violin. Their music introduced great violinists to the world, and subsequently works were created for these violinists. This tradition first began with Francesco Geminiani and reached a high point with Niccolò Paganini—the legacy continues into the 20th and 21st centuries with Yehudi Menuhin, Isaac Stern, Josh Bell, and Anne-Sophie Mutter, among others.

As musical performances and venues changed, and the 19th century ushered in the solo violinist and the auditorium, the violin evolved still further. The intimate tone of the Baroque 18th-century violin was exchanged for a louder tone produced by a taller bridge, a thicker soundpost and bass bar, an angled-back neck, and a flatter body. These changes resulted in greater pressure on the strings against the bridge, which meant the violin lost its delicate, quiet tone.

The violin found its way early on into the folk music and cultures of many countries. The Middle East, southern India, Europe, and Latin America took up the sound of this versatile instrument. Today the violin is heard in everything from rock 'n' roll music to historical performances to Latin jazz.

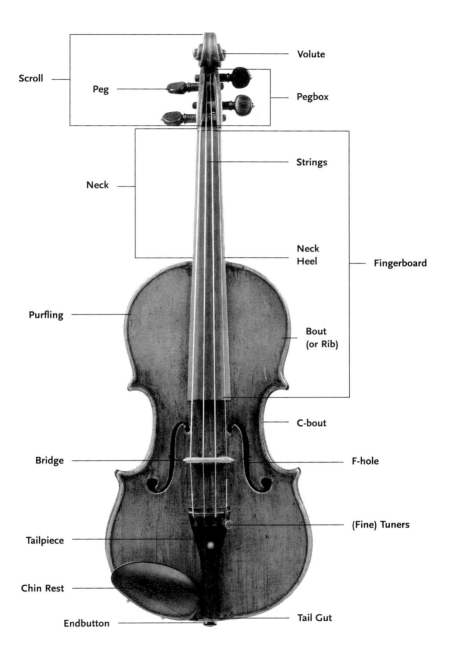

Volute

Scroll

Peg

Pegbox

Strings

Neck

Neck
Heel

Fingerboard

Purfling

Bout
(or Rib)

C-bout

Bridge

F-hole

(Fine) Tuners

Tailpiece

Chin Rest

Endbutton

Tail Gut

FACE VALUE: WHO BUILT THIS VIOLIN?

by James N. McKean

Sometimes it seems as though in every attic in America, there is a violin waiting to be discovered. In Europe, I would expect there to be two; and in the average castle, even three or four. The inevitable discovery (usually the consequence of settling an estate) almost always leads to difficulties, because it is a rare family that doesn't think that somewhere in its late relative's attic is a work of art or an heirloom that will make the appraisers from Christie's faint at the sight of it.

The object of fond hopes for attic raiders and treasure hunters is likely to be the violin. The case itself invites romance—old and worn, redolent of rosin and varnish. Looking at it, the lone searcher among the detritus remembers having read a story—a lost Stradivari discovered—and breathlessly lifts the instrument from the case. The family gazes in excitement and awe at what they have found: their own Stradivari. How do they know? The label says so.

WHAT A LABEL REALLY SAYS

When an instrument is sold, its price is determined primarily by who built it—and you might think the label is the best place to look for that information. But that is the last thing an expert will take into consideration when trying to determine the authorship of any particular violin. That might sound odd, since every instrument, even the most humble, has a piece of paper glued to the inside back. Visible through the bass soundhole, the label carries the maker's name and, usually, the city in which he worked—as well as the year the instrument was made. (Some makers went so far as to include their street address and patron saint.) However, many makers, even those as illustrious as the Goffrillers, the Ruggieris, and the lesser Guarneris, apparently let many instruments go out of their shops unlabeled. In virtually every case, that regrettable oversight has been corrected at some point in the intervening centuries.

It should be pointed out that the belief in a label is for most a well-founded cultural response. Everything around us is labeled—try shopping for something that is not. But, when identifying violins, the last thing you want to look at is the label. Not because they're frequently wrong; in fact, in the vast majority of cases, they are original to the instrument. But that doesn't mean that the name on the label is the same as that of the man who made what you're holding. The fact is that the insertion of fraudulent labels is almost as old as the violin itself. One of the earliest documents we have relating to violins is a letter of complaint. A violinist named Vitali writes an indignant petition for redress to the Duke of Moderna. Vitali bought a violin for 12 pistoles, believing that it was what the label read, a fine Amati. Under that label, though, he finds another—that of the true author of the work, a member of the Ruggieri family. The violin is only worth a fourth of what he paid, and this was in 1685—within a year of Nicolò Amati's death, and only 55 miles from Cremona (for a more detailed look at the practice of labeling instruments, the Hills devote an entire chapter to the subject in their books *Antonio Stradivari, His Life and His Work*

A clear distinction is made between outright fraud and the making of a replica, where there is no intent to deceive. A maker may insert a replica label after copying a classic model.

(2nd edition, Dover Publications, New York) and *The Violin-Makers of the Guarneri Family* (Reprint edition, Dover Publications, New York).)

An important distinction must be made between outright fraud and the making of replica, where there is no intent to deceive. There is a long and perfectly respectable tradition of inserting a replica label if a classic maker's model is being used. The great 19th-century maker and dealer J.B. Vuillaume did so with his copies of Stradivaris and Guarneris. W.E. Hill & Sons have examined many instruments deciphering labels and believe they have two violins with such double labels thought to have been inserted by Ruggieri himself. But it wasn't fraud Ruggieri had in mind, it was the rationale of the maker that a reproduction of an Amati (or a Stradivari, or a Stainer) was not complete without a reproduction label.

PROVING PROVENANCE

Unfortunately, there is no objective way to establish authorship of a piece, short of having a photograph of the maker holding it. Considering that the most valuable works were created long before Daguerre was born, that idea presents problems. The next best thing is to trace the ownership of the instrument—its provenance—as far back as possible. Ideally, one would have an unbroken record of owners reaching back to the original patron. But this is almost never the case, particularly when dealing with Italian instruments of the 18th century and earlier. It's easy to see why: while some luthiers might have kept records of where their instruments went, no one subsequently ever thought such records were worth keeping, for none survive. Almost all the buyers exercised the same casual attitude, which reveals something of the light in which the craft must have been viewed at the time; few were aware that they were trafficking in what would someday be priceless antiques. Aside from Amati and Stradivari, internationally famous in their own day, the instruments of the classical Italian makers did not achieve any particular status until the end of the 18th century—long enough for them to have changed hands many times. It is generally only after they surfaced in England or France, usually in the 19th century, that any chain of ownership was established.

An example of labels thought to have been used by Antonio Stradivari.

Over the years, and particularly in the past few decades, the antique instruments business has come to rely almost entirely on certificates to establish authenticity. When there is no record of manufacture and no chain of ownership, all that is left is the weight of expert opinion. Connoisseurs, through broad exposure, gain a familiarity that allows them to "zero in" on the maker of an instrument or bow. They begin with national characteristics and consider different periods; they then look for details that would tie the origin to a more specific area—Cremona, for instance, or Paris. At that point, there might be features that are peculiar to a school of making, such as that of Amati or Gagliano. Finally, one hopes to find those touches that betray the hand of a known maker, for example the slight extra half-turn on a Seraphin scroll or the way Maggini undercut his f-holes. An expert will gain an affinity for a maker's tool-handling style, his way of looking at wood—these details add up to an artist's signature and are as distinctive as handwriting.

Over the years, and particularly in the past few decades, the antique instruments business has come to rely almost entirely on certificates to establish authenticity.

However, experts whose opinions have stood the test of time—Rembert Wurlitzer, for example, or W.E. Hill & Sons—proved to have had not just unfailing eyes but also trusted judgments. Being able to single out the real thing means nothing if people have no faith in the expert's honesty. While Rembert Wurlitzer certificates carry a tremendous weight, those of the Rudolph Wurlitzer Co. have very little value because their resident expert, Jay C. Freeman, is notorious for having gotten away with what he could. The situation also points out a peculiarity of the violin business: the certificates used to authenticate an instrument or bow have almost always been issued by someone selling them—not, one would think, the best way to get an honest opinion.

Relying unquestioningly on papers can lead to an expensive mistake. Major firms began attaching photographs to their certificates in the early 1920s. They did so, no doubt, to foil unscrupulous dealers who used the papers to validate fakes, while at the same time selling the genuine article on its own merits. This practice has been taken a step further by the wonders of modern technology—I was once offered a violin purported to be a Panormo, on the basis of a photocopy of a Hill certificate that didn't have photographs. The fact that the body length was off by an eighth of an inch was laid to shrinkage or sloppy work. In this case, three violins could have been on the market—the first, the genuine Panormo with another cer-

tificate; a forgery with the original Hill paper; and another forgery with a photocopy of the Hill paper.

The practice of labeling itself is not confined to only top-of-the-line antique reproductions—it is observed in every category of instrument, down to the cheapest boxes slammed together in the factories of Mirecourt and Klingental. The labels in these production-line instruments aren't even a close attempt to reproduce the original; all they are meant to do is indicate the model used—a necessary step, since usually the instrument is so poorly made that the model is barely recognizable.

Many people, overcome by the excitement of finding their own Stradivari in the attic, fail to notice the fine print, frequently, "made in Czechoslovakia" or "*nach* Stradivari" (*nach* is German for "after"). Every maker or dealer has participated in the following conversation: when the non-Italian location is pointed out, the finder of the instrument, reluctant to give up hope, suggests that perhaps Stradivari made it while on vacation or at his country house. Never mind that Czechoslovakia, or for that matter Germany, came into being more than a century after he died.

FAKE YOUR OWN LABEL

Several years ago I decided to make an antique violin. I did so for several reasons: I wanted to see how my varnish would wear over time; successful antiquing presents a special challenge to a maker's skill; and, hardly least of all, antiques sell more readily and for more money than brand-new instruments (proving yet again that people are more than willing to pay for their prejudices). Not being interested in copying a maker or a specific instrument—who wants to be a human Xerox machine?—I created a maker, Gattopardo (the Leopard). You've never heard of him; he lived in Parma and worked around 1700—at least that is the evidence provided by the labels on the two instruments known to us.

I wanted the label in the violin to have the same feel as the rest of it, so the materials were important. There's nothing like the real thing for a successful fake: luckily, the prospective owner of the instrument also happened to be a dealer in rare antique maps, and he had a supply of paper and parchment that was centuries old. You can use regular ink sold in an art store for wood-block prints, as I did; or if you want to go the limit, you can mix up an ink that is genuinely faux with some lampblack and shellac. Most 18th-century labels were printed with movable-type blocks—only a few, such as that of Sanctus Seraphin, an Italian maker, used engraved copperplate—and so the lettering is impressed into the paper. Fake labels done on a copier are fairly easy to spot, because even though any paper can now be used, the lettering is heat-transferred and therefore has a characteristic raised appearance.

I also needed the handmade look of 18th-century lettering. The best place to find it was, needless to say, on a label of the period. I had a wealth of them to choose from—there are several dictionaries that provide page after page of photographs of labels from some of the most obscure makers. Testore turned out to be the man for me: his label has so much printed on it that there were more than enough letters to get what I needed. I photocopied the label at the correct size, and after a little work with a sharp knife and some Elmer's glue, and I had what I wanted: "Gattopardo in Parma."

I took it to a stamp maker. He made me a rubber stamp, which I promptly discarded. What I needed was what he was going to throw away—the metal slug used to make the stamp. This was my printing block. I taped the paper in a vise, inked up the slug with a breyer (roller), and then pressed out the label. A fountain pen (you can use a felt-tipped one, but it won't look just right) for the date, and there it was: an authentic fake label from 1709.

So, if you're shopping for an antique violin, don't give much weight to the label, or even to the paperwork. The most important thing you can do is find a respectable dealer, and buy from someone you can trust. Be sure to have an expert research the instrument's provenance and authenticate any certificates or photographs before making an investment.

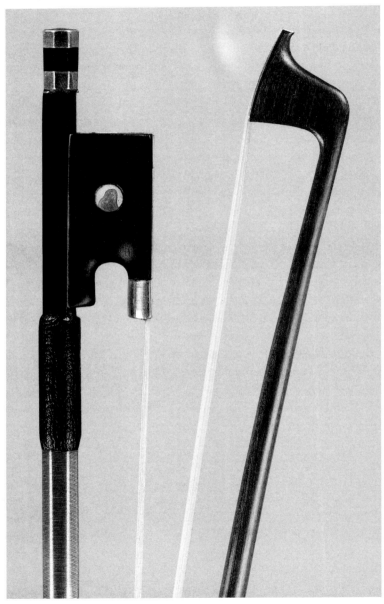

French bows—such as this one made by Dominique Pecatte—are favored by musicians and collectors alike.

WHAT IS A BOW?

by James N. McKean

Your instrument's bow is deceptively simple: a stick of wood and a frog to hold the hair. The bow reached its final form much later than the violin; it was not until the beginning of the 19th century, in Paris, that François Tourte perfected the design (see The Evolution of the Bow, page 18). The stick, for anything better than the cheapest grade of bow, is almost always made from a tropical hardwood called pernambuco. It is an extremely dense wood—like ebony, it sinks in water—but it combines flexibility with great strength and durability. The bow maker graduates the stick in precise gradations (according to Tourte's system) so that it is evenly flexible throughout. The ideal bow allows the musician to draw a full stroke from frog to tip without feeling the slightest change in the way it grabs the string; it should also bounce quickly and evenly in spiccato passages.

The maker achieves the camber, or curve, of the bow by heating it over a flame and bending it. The shape and distribution of the camber are critical to your bow's performance, and altering them is an art. The weight of the bow falls within narrow parameters, with a variance of a few grams at most, and the balance point must also be precisely located for the bow to feel right. Contrary to what many people believe, the strength of the bow does not depend on its weight; French bows, which, in the antique market, are still considered the best, tend to be light. Much more important than weight are the balance and evenness of response. The selection of a bow is intensely personal—it has to match both you as a player and your instrument—and there is no question that the bow you use will affect the quality of sound you get from your instrument. As with instruments, the perception still exists that older bows are better, but certainly there are bows being made today that, in materials, skill of workmanship, and pure artistry, rival any from the past.

The bow's frog is usually ebony, although traditionally, when bow makers have wanted to "dress up" a bow they consider better than average, they have used ivory

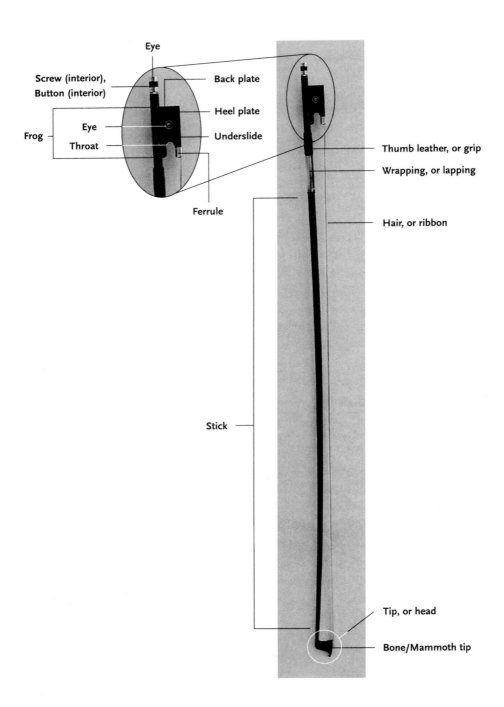

Eye

Screw (interior),
Button (interior)

Back plate

Heel plate

Frog

Eye

Underslide

Throat

Ferrule

Thumb leather, or grip

Wrapping, or lapping

Hair, or ribbon

Stick

Tip, or head

Bone/Mammoth tip

or tortoiseshell. Since both these materials come from endangered species, their use and importation are now banned. Makers use substitutes for the frog, as well as for the ivory tip and the black-and-white whalebone lapping that protects the lower end of the stick from wear from the forefinger. Mastodon tusk—often dug out of the Arctic ice—serves for ivory, while artificial resins have provided a reasonable substitute for tortoiseshell and whalebone. The lapping, as well as the tip, can also be of silver; the choice depends as much on weight and balance as personal preference. Between the lapping and the front of the frog is a wrapping called the grip, which is made of either leather or snakeskin.

The frequency with which you will have to rehair your bow will vary, but you will want to have it changed at least once a year.

The bow hair is knotted at each end and then inserted into cavities in the head and the frog, where it is held in place by fitted wooden plugs. A slide fits into the bottom of the frog; this is traditionally faced with abalone, sometimes of a wild pattern. As with the neck of the instrument, the slide frequently is not the original, and whether it is or not has no effect on the value. The other metal parts of the bow—the ferrule (the small semicircle covering the protruding tongue of the frog that holds the hair), the button, and the circles (if the bow has them) around the inlaid eyes on the sides of the frog—can be gold instead of silver, again marking a bow of extra merit. On more inexpensive bows, this metal is usually nickel.

The frog is held in place by a small screw that extends inside the end of the stick and is turned by the button. The screw goes through a threaded eyelet, which is attached to the frog; you can see it if you unscrew the button all the way (but be sure that the hair is not twisted before you screw it all back together).

MINIMIZING YOUR BOW'S WEAR

You'll find it relatively easy to maintain your bow and minimize the wear from even constant use. The frequency with which you will have to rehair the bow will vary, but at least once a year you will want to have it changed, if not more often (many professionals who "play hard" get their bows rehaired several times during the season). If the bow starts losing its traction on the strings, it's time to get new hair. It's a common misperception that the hair is covered with tiny scales that grab the string; while the hair is rough, it's the rosin that creates the friction and thus the sound. But too much rosin is as bad as none at all; it can build up very fast and clog

Too much rosin is as bad as none at all; it can build up very fast and clog both the hair and the strings.

both the hair and the strings, in addition to drifting down onto the top of your instrument, where it will build up and harden like old snowdrifts. Another old trick that doesn't really work is cleaning the hair with alcohol to remove the rosin buildup. This can play serious havoc with the finish on the bow, no matter how careful you are, and doesn't do anything to revive the bite of the hair on the strings.

The length of the hair is very important. Sensitive to changes in humidity, it will stretch in the summer, to the point where often it needs to be shortened. You should never have to turn the button more than three or four times to get the proper tension to play—and when it is fully loosened, the hair should not be so loose it touches the stick, or sags like an old ribbon. It should stay straight. The danger is that if the hair is too long, when it is brought to proper tension your thumb will hit the stick between the frog and the leather grip. Even though pernambuco is one of the hardest and most durable woods known to man, you will be amazed at how quickly you can wear a deep dent in the side of the stick. It can be repaired, but it will weaken the stick and lessen its value. For the same reason, keep an eye on the leather grip, and when it gets worn down to the point you can see the winding or the wood underneath, have it replaced right away. Dryness can have its effects too; if the hair is already short, a

Leaving your bow lying across an open violin case can lead to disaster—this is a common cause of severe bow damage.

sudden dry spell can shrink the hair enough to pop the head off. Always loosen the hair after playing, and if the hair seems to be too long, have it shortened.

Rehairing time is also a good time to have the overall condition checked. On a bow, minute defects can become huge problems, resulting in major devaluation of the bow (a broken head devalues a bow by 90 percent). A crack in the ivory headplate, if not repaired, can result in the head splitting from the pressure of the plug that holds the hair in place. If the button won't turn easily, don't force it—there is something binding inside, and you should have it looked at.

Like your instrument, the bow is remarkably durable and needs only a modicum of attention to keep it in top shape.

PROTECT YOUR BOW

Most damage to bows comes from being careless. Don't under any circumstances leave the bow lying across the violin in an open case—the lid can and often does fall. The bow will almost certainly end up with serious damage, but it can also injure the instrument in the process. Securing the bow and closing the case is an excellent idea, anyway. Bows have an alarming ability to disappear—they are easily transportable, and to any but the practiced eye they all look the same. Zip the case while you're at it—you might forget that you haven't and pick it up and then the instrument will come tumbling out.

THE EVOLUTION
OF THE BOW

by Yung Chin

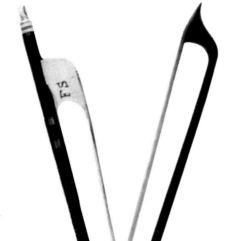

This early violin bow displays the distinctive piked tip and slightly convex camber associated with transitional bows.

The bow as we know it took centuries to evolve into its present form. From the mid 1600s to the late 1700s, bows changed in size, length, balance, and shape, along with the evolving musical forms and compositional styles in various countries. In France during the mid 1600s, bows used for dance music were short, with a slightly convex camber. In Italy, bows used for sonatas and concerts were long and straight, also with a slightly convex camber. And in Germany, bows were somewhat shorter and firmer than in Italy, in part because they were used to play Germanic polyphonic music.

The early instrumental concerto, or concerto grosso, was developed mainly by Italian composers of the 17th and 18th centuries, during the Baroque era. The concerto grosso consisted of a string ensemble with a solo instrument—usually the flute, oboe, or violin—and balanced interplay between soloist and orchestra. Some of the music of Corelli, Vivaldi, and Geminiani was representative of this style. In the Classic concerto, the piano was more often the solo instrument, and the balance between soloist and orchestra changed. The orchestra provided accompaniment for a series of virtuosic displays by the solo instrument, and the cadenza became highly developed. The concertos of Paganini, Vieuxtemps, and later Wieniawski typified this musical style. These works called for a firmer and quicker responding bow for ricochet, up-and-down staccato, spiccato, and more articulate martelé strokes.

At the middle of the 17th century in France, the woods used for stringed-instrument bows were predominantly European, light, and quite flexible. But tropical woods began to show up in parts of Europe in the early 1500s. Pernambuco wood, from Brazil, would become the primary wood used by French bow makers from the early to middle 1700s. Trade in pernambuco lasted from about 1550 to 1840. Today, pernambuco supplies have severely dwindled, and many bow makers are exploring other options.

THE TRANSITIONAL BOW

In the mid 1600s to the early 1700s, the head of the bow was of a piked design (pointed like a Baroque bow), and the frog height was lowered. The camber of the bow became slightly convex, and the hair fitted into place going from the head of the bow back to the frog and around the back of the frog onto the stick. The frog was then put into position to achieve proper tension. There was no use of a metal ferrule on the frog at this time, and the moveable frog tightened by a button does not surface until much later. This was known as the Corelli bow, and with it a musician could play chords and utilize certain bow strokes more easily. But it was not as easy to sustain a full, rich sound. In the mid 1700s, the so-called Tartini bow came of age. It was longer than the Corelli bow, and the fluting at the lower end made it even easier to handle. Then in about 1760, the Cramer bow was developed. Named after German violinist Wilhelm Cramer, the new bow head was pointed in the front and the back. The frog height was lower, and, most important, the stick had a slight concave curve to it. The Cramer bow became the bridge between the transitional bows of the time and the later, more modern Tourte design.

The advent of the increasingly larger concert hall in the late 18th and 19th centuries had a great impact on the violin, and consequently, the bow. The hall required stronger tonal power and wider dynamic range, which, in the case of the violin, was achieved through more bow tension. A firmer bow was required to draw a fuller sound from the violin. The choice of wood and the concave camber of the bow also had an effect on the sound. With a dense wood such as pernambuco, the bow could be strong and still retain some of the flexibility required to attain a good sound. More camber in the bow gave it a firmer feel and a quicker articulation on certain bow strokes.

THE MODERN BOW AND ITS EVOLUTION

Between 1770 and 1785, the modern bow was perfected by the Tourte family in con-
junction with the influence of players—particularly Giovanni Battista Viotti
(1755–1824), the greatest violinist of his time. It is said that François Xavier Tourte
was to the bow what Stradivari was to the violin. But perhaps Tourte was even more
important to his respective craft—from the point of innovation—than was
Stradivari. Born in 1848, Tourte lived most of his 87 years in Paris, where he had
direct contact with the great players of his day. Historically, luthiers worked closely with leading players of their time, and although the bow makers of Mirecourt and
Markneukirchen rarely traveled the world, their bows did. Thus bow makers could
see what their counterparts in other cities and countries were doing.

The Tourte family has had a profound impact on bow making both in its own
time and in the present. François Tourte (1748–1835) and his brother Nicolas
Leonard Tourte (1746–1807) perfected the overall basic form of today's bow, including its length (72.5 cm), graduations, camber, and proportions (head and frog).
During the Tourte era, generally the heads were on the high side, the frogs were
long, and the stick had little camber.

After Tourte, the next influential maker was Dominique Peccatte (1810–74), who
studied bow making in J.B. Vuillaume's shop from 1826 to 1837; he probably
learned from Jean Pierre Persios (1808–60) and, perhaps, Claude Joseph Fonclouse
(1799–1862). In 1837, Peccatte took over François Lupot's shop, and in 1848 he

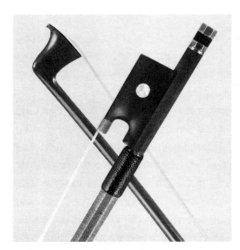

returned to Mirecourt, where he lived
the rest of his life. He influenced
Nicolas Maire (1800–74), Nicolas
Maline (1822–77), and Joseph Henry
(1823–70), to name a few. Peccatte
was not a great technical maker, but
he more than made up for that with
the overall beauty of his bows. During
his era, bow heads tended to be lower,
and there was more camber than in
the bows of Tourte's time.

The early bows of François Nicolas
Voirin (1833–85) were based on a
Peccatte model; later he developed the
smaller, round head now associated

A silver-mounted violin bow by Eugène Sartory.

with him. He was prolific and maintained a very precise level of style and technique. The camber of the
later Voirin bows also became more pronounced, especially behind the head. Voirin was perhaps the most
influential French maker of the second half of the 19th
century, although some of his contemporaries, such as
Maire and Peccatte, expressed more stylistic freedom
in their work.

German bow makers, such as Ludwig Christian
Bausch (1805–85), the Knopf family, and in particular
Carl Heinrich Knopf (1839–75), made wonderful bows.
The Nurnberger family, especially Franz Albert
Nurnberger Sr. (1826–94) and Karl Albert Nurnberger
(1885–1971) also made beautiful Tourte-inspired violin
bows (as well as cello bows). Hermann Richard
Pfretzschner (1856–1925) made some Voirin-inspired

During the time that François
and Nicolas Leonard Tourte
were making bows, the tips
were on the high side.

bows, which in craftsmanship are very hard to distinguish from the real Voirin bow
(when looking at the bow head). In their best work, some of the better German bow
makers were certainly the equal of many French makers. And not to be overlooked,
English bow makers such as members of the Todd and Tubbs families produced
high-quality bows.

THE IMPACT OF SCHOOLS
AND PLAYING STYLES ON BOW DESIGN

Performers, teachers, and schools of playing have always had an impact on the
kinds of bows and instruments people have chosen. The Italian school of playing
included Arcangelo Corelli (1653–1713), Giuseppe Tartini (1652–1770), Gaetano
Pugnani (1727–1803), and of course Niccolò Paganini (1784–1840). The French
school included Jean-Marie Leclair (1697–1764), and later Rudolf Kreutzer
(1766–1831) and Pierre Rode (1774–1830). Among the influential German players
were Ludwig Spohr (1784–1859), Ferdinand David (1810–73), and Joseph Joachim
(1831–1907).

In the 1800s, the Franco-Belgian school came of age with Charles-Auguste de
Bériot (1820–81) and later Eugène Ysaÿe (1858–1931), who was known for his development of vibrato. Near the end of the 19th century, the classic Russian school of

playing began to take hold. Its most influential figure was Leopold Auer (1845–1930), and his students, including Mischa Elman, Toscha Seidel, Nathan Milstein, Jascha Heifetz, and Efrem Zimbalist. An American school of playing, based on some of the Franco-Belgian and classic Russian styles, has held sway for the past 40 to 50 years. One of its best-known teachers was Ivan Galamian (1903–81). A characteristic of his teaching was a firmer bow grip, with the index finger more extended, leading to firmer contact between the bow hair and string. This grip requires a more rigid bow (although if the grip is exaggerated, the freedom of sound may be lost). Generally speaking, such bows are heavier, with denser wood; the frog and head heights are lower; and the camber is quite full, especially behind the head of the bow. Eugène Sartory (1871–1946) was one of numerous makers following Voirin's era whose bows fit this description.

Sartory was also quite prolific and considered the most important maker of the first half of the 20th century. He apprenticed with Charles Peccatte and Alfred Lamy, and his own early bows show Lamy's influence, while his later bows became heavier in execution and style. Some of the bows of Sartory's contemporaries, such as those of the Lamy family, and of Claude Thomassin (1865–1942), were more sought after by players during the first half of the century, but today the style of playing has changed and there is a greater demand for the Sartory bow. A very good, plain, ebony-and-silver mounted Sartory can sell for about $15,000, while a very good Vigneron or Thomassin sells for about $7,000–$10,000.

Next time you pick up your bow, pause for a moment and think about how the bow has evolved over the years. Each generation of bow makers learned from the previous one. Reflecting the collective efforts of several generations of makers, the bow continues to develop and serve the many needs of stringed-instrument musicians.

WHAT DO THE BASS BAR
AND SOUNDPOST DO?

by James N. McKean

The bridge might be the heart of your instrument, but the soundpost is the soul. The French, in fact, call it the *âme*—their word for soul. When you tune your violin to pitch, the strings exert approximately 40 pounds of pressure on the top through the feet of the bridge. Spruce, the wood the top is made of, has one of the best strength-to-weight ratios of any natural material, but at its thickest point the violin top measures less than 3 mm. (The cello's top, in spite of its vastly larger area and the greater pressure exerted by the strings, is not much thicker, measuring less than

Setting the soundpost, a simple-looking piece of wood, is an exacting task, one of the most difficult in violin making.

5 mm.) Forty pounds of pressure is much more than $\frac{1}{16}$th of an inch of spruce could withstand on its own, regardless of its stellar strength ratio. The top would have to be a good half inch thick to handle that pressure unaided, which would produce an instrument with about as much sound as a practice violin with a mute on it. How does it avoid collapsing, then? Look through the f-holes and you'll see—there's a support under each bridge foot. On the treble side you'll find the soundpost, a dowel of spruce wedged between the top and the back, while just visible inside the upper eye of the other f-hole is the bass bar.

THE SOUNDPOST

While the soundpost might seem to be no more than a simple stick of wood, getting one to fit correctly is an exacting task—one of the most difficult in the craft. The ends of the post are cut at a slant to match the tapering of the body, and the difference between a post that fits and one that doesn't can be as little as a shaving. A soundpost that doesn't match the taper of the instrument can do serious damage to the inside of the top, for the edges are sharp and if they don't fit exactly, they can easily dent or tear the top. Although spruce is uncommonly strong, its side grain—the surface that the post rests against—is very soft. On the other hand, the part of the post that meets the top is end grain, which is very hard. Think about chewing on a pencil and how easy it is to mark it up; your teeth on the cedar pencil have about the same effect as an ill-fitting post on the unprotected wood of the top (or the back; over time, an ill-fitting post can even dent maple). And if the post is not standing perfectly straight, the sharp edges of even the most well-fitted post can cause harm.

Aside from its purely structural use in holding up the top, the soundpost plays a role in the acoustics of your instrument.

Aside from its purely structural use in holding up the top, the soundpost plays a role in the acoustics of your instrument. When you draw the bow, the sound waves travel through the bridge to the body, which acts as an amplifier. The violin is often compared to the human voice, and with good reason; the violin is the instrument that comes closest to producing as many overtones as you hear when you're listening to a singer. But since a vibrating string by itself is inaudible, the instrument has to amplify all the complex overtones and harmonics produced by the string when you bow it. The wood not only vibrates, it also moves; as the bow pulls the string, the bridge rocks, which moves the top up and down. The soundpost acts like a plunger, transmitting this movement to the back. Where the post sits relative to the bridge will directly affect the way the sound waves from the string and the motion of the bridge are transmitted to the back.

THE BASS BAR

The bass bar, another of your instrument's vital organs, is a strip of spruce that is fitted and glued to the top on the bass side. It serves the same dual role as the soundpost: supporting the top and at the same time helping to distribute the vibrations emanating from the bridge when you play the instrument. The bass bar acts like a spring under the bass leg of the bridge as it rocks back and forth, adding more vibration to the natural resonance of the body of the instrument. Because most of the sound produced by the lower strings comes from the vibration of the top plate, it is of the utmost importance that the bar be properly positioned and shaped. It has to be right before the body is closed up; once the top is on, the bar is out of reach.

The bar itself is fashioned from a piece of spruce, preferably split (rather than sawn) from the billet to assure the straightest possible grain and therefore the most strength. It is then fitted, by plane and knife, so that it conforms exactly to the con-

The bass bar is fitted by plane and knife to conform exactly to the shape of the violin top. It acts like a spring, adding vibration to the violin's natural resonance.

The bass bar, another of your instrument's vital organs, is a strip of spruce that is fitted and glued to the top on the bass side.

tours of the top. If it doesn't fit perfectly, the flexible top will deform itself as necessary to match an imperfectly set bar.

Fitting can be a tricky undertaking because the interior surface of the top of an older instrument is, more often than not, quite irregular. To make the fitting even more difficult, the bar is sprung in with tension—which means that, when fitting it, a gap of a few millimeters is left at each end. The result is that when the bar is glued in, it raises the top slightly—so that when the instrument is strung up, the top will settle back down under the pressure of the bridge to the shape in which it was cut. This is another aspect of the art that goes into making a bar; every violin maker has his or her own opinion about how much tension is necessary and how it should be distributed.

While your instrument has a fundamental voice that can't be changed, the soundpost and the bassbar have a decided effect on the balance and timbre of the sound.

CHOOSE THE RIGHT TOOLS

Considering your goals as a player before you go shopping will help you focus your search.

CONSIDERING YOUR FIRST GOOD INSTRUMENT

by Susan M. Barbieri

After conquering the "Bach double" last year, I knew I was ready. I'd logged three years of work as an adult beginner on the violin and was playing first violin in a string quartet. My student instrument was starting to sound shrill under my ear, sluggish under my hand, and too bright to blend with the quartet. It was time to step up.

With a rough budget in mind, I visited a reputable dealer and began the winnowing process. I played about a half dozen fine instruments and quickly narrowed to two the violins I would take home and bring to my lesson. One was a lovely sounding violin costing $4,000; the other, which I'd begun calling "the Chicago" because of where it was made, cost about $2,000. I was leaning toward the less expensive instrument, which had the rich, silky tone and effortless response I wanted. But I wasn't sure, so without telling my teacher or friends the prices, I conducted blind "taste tests" to get listeners' opinions.

Each time, "the Chicago," the less expensive instrument, won out—prompting "oohs" and "aahs" from teachers and friends. I couldn't be happier with my beautiful violin.

An instrument-buying experience can be fairly straightforward and stress-free, but not every beginning- to intermediate-level musician has an easy time making that first step up. For many, the process of buying a good stringed instrument is an agonizing one. But with the right preparation and the right attitude, experts say, it does not have to be. The key to making a good decision lies in asking the right questions of yourself, of the instrument seller, and of those who are closest to you musically.

ASKING THE RIGHT QUESTIONS

How do you know when you're ready to move on to your first good instrument? Susan Leek-Dedon, who teaches at the University of St. Thomas Conservatory and sells instruments part-time for Miller and Fein Violins in St. Paul, Minnesota, says that usually an $800 student instrument will hold a player for a few years—whether he or she is a young student or an adult beginner.

"This is especially true at beginner levels. You're still learning how to hold the bow. But once you get to a certain level, you start to outgrow your instrument," says Leek-Dedon, who has taught for more than 20 years.

"For instance, when you're trying to play a passage, it may not be as clear as you think it should be because the instrument doesn't respond. And when you're going up in position, again, it's not doing what you want. Another telltale sign is, 'Wow, I'm hunkered down on my bow arm but it's just not giving me the power I want—even though I'm doing everything my teacher tells me to do.'"

Once you know you're ready for a new instrument, it's important to consider your goals as a player before you actually go shopping. Claire Givens, owner of Claire Givens Violins in Minneapolis, asks prospective buyers to consider how their instrument will be used. In a hall? In a church? Are you a young prodigy or an adult amateur playing for your own enjoyment?

"Figure all that out. Then go into it with an absolutely open mind about sound and response," Givens says. "People get the best instrument when they come in and *don't* say, 'I want something old' or 'I really like brown violins' or 'I was told to stay away from French instruments.' Instead, they come in and say, 'I really want to experience every one of these instruments and see what they can do for me.'"

SETTING A BUDGET

People often ask Givens about pricing. She says there are four things that go into pricing any instrument: authenticity, quality of craftsmanship, condition, and sound. First-time buyers won't be able to determine authenticity and quality of workmanship, but Givens says that if you do business with a reputable dealer, you can get a crash course in how to listen and how to look at the condition of an instrument.

How much to spend depends on a lot of things, Leek-Dedon agrees, but as a general rule she advises that it's reasonable to double or triple the value on your first step up from a beginning instrument to a quality instrument. "I had a young woman come into the shop who had been playing less than a year," she recalls. "She was not that good, but she showed good coordination, had a good ear, and probably could do well with it in the future. She had been told by a public school teacher that she should spend $3,000 or $4,000 on her first instrument. I said, 'Well, I think that's really high.' Sure, I'd like to sell a more expensive instrument. But sometimes you place yourself with a too-expensive instrument and you're not ready for it."

WHERE TO PURCHASE YOUR INSTRUMENT

Several experts warn against trying to buy your first good instrument at an auction, although prices there may be low. As St. Paul instrument maker and dealer John Waddle points out, an auction house's viewing room will be big and unfamiliar, with lots of other people playing and talking. You're not going to have sufficient time, they're not going to let you take the instrument out for a week and try it, and no follow-up services will be provided.

Buy from someone who has a selection of instruments for you to view if and when you decide to trade up.

Teacher commissions can be another potential pitfall for the unwary or uninformed buyer. Some dealers pay teachers who help students pick out an instrument from their shop. The commission is usually a percentage of the sale price of the instrument. Not all shops and teachers engage in the practice, and when the buyer is informed that a commission is being paid, there is nothing unethical about a teacher being reimbursed for the time and effort he or she puts into helping a student make a difficult choice. But buyers should be aware that in some cases commissions are paid without their knowledge, and then the objectivity of the teacher's advice can legitimately be questioned.

Even putting aside the question of teacher commissions, Mark Bjork, a professor of violin and pedagogy in the University of Minnesota's music department, advises buyers to take their teacher's opinion into account, but never to neglect their own feelings about it. He recalls his own experience with a student who was trying to decide between two violins.

"I had had a chance to try them before she did, and they were both very nice examples, but one of them, I felt, was much better sounding than the other one. She came in after a week or so of trying them and said she had made her decision, and it was not the instrument I would have chosen. And I was a little bit surprised until

I heard her play them. She sounded very much better on the one that she had chosen. I didn't, but she did," Bjork says.

Bjork adds that students should consider instruments being made by contemporary makers because of their high quality as well as the fact that old instruments frequently are out of the shopper's price range. In fact, he adds, sometimes a top-of-the-line mass-produced instrument will be better than a bad handmade one.

But if he believes the student will run up against certain limitations with a particular instrument, Bjork doesn't hesitate to point that out. And if he sees a student leaning toward something that he thinks is going to be a bad investment, he says so. Bjork believes it's important to think of that first good instrument as an investment. He advises students to buy from a reputable dealer who will give them a good trade-in policy on the one that they're purchasing. Buy from someone who is apt to have a selection of things for you to view if and when you do decide to trade up, he says.

But according to Waddle, some shoppers seem excessively worried about investment value. "Many people understand investment value more than they understand sound," he says. His view is that in the lower price ranges, say $2,000 and under for a violin, you're not going to get an investment instrument. So you need to decide how important that is to you.

Waddle always tells people to sit down and figure out a comfortable price range, then look at instruments within that range and call and make an appointment with the instrument maker or dealer. Tell him or her your price range. That way, the maker or dealer can have several appropriate choices ready for you to try. (Givens adds that it is helpful to bring in your present instrument and bow to give the shop owner an idea of what you are accustomed to hearing.) Then begins the process of testing and narrowing down the choices.

HOW BEST TO SHOP FOR YOUR NEXT VIOLIN

Leek-Dedon has three criteria she asks prospective buyers to think about when they come into the shop: How clear and responsive is the instrument? How do you like the sound? Is it comfortable to play or does your hand become fatigued?

A common mistake, Waddle says, is that shoppers set forth without a plan. Be organized. Know what you're going to play and do it fairly quickly. "I don't recommend practicing in the shop," he says. "And don't try to impress the other people in the shop with your playing. I can't tell you how many people I've had pick up the violin, launch into the Tchaikovsky violin concerto, and about two bars into it realize the violin is not in tune."

Another problem, Waddle has observed, is that very shy, young players who come in with their parents are frequently afraid and don't know what to do. "They need to say to themselves, 'OK, I'm going to play a G-major scale, I'm going to start on the G string, I'm going to play all the way up to the E string, then I'm going to play a simple piece, maybe a slow piece, and then I'm going to play a fast piece.' You need to pick a violin up, do that process, and put it down. It doesn't need to take more than an hour to try six violins."

"People can only keep a sound in their mind for a few seconds," says Givens. "So don't play long excerpts. That way, you can sense a contrast immediately. As you get more practice, you can retain the effect of sound and the memory of sound longer, but at first, ten or 15 seconds might be it. I line up four instruments at a time, max. And I put shoulder rests on every single one so they're ready to just pick up, put under the chin, and play. I ask the shopper to narrow those four instruments down to two or one. Then I bring in some more. And I keep doing that until it's impossible to be discriminating. And I try to get people to move ahead as much as possible, quickly, because for about 20 minutes you have your maximum concentration. After that, it's really hard work to remember and discriminate and focus."

Givens also tries to help people develop a vocabulary to use in evaluating instruments. You're going to get your best help if you can develop the words to communicate what you're experiencing. "This one's too bright," for instance. "This one's too edgy." "I don't like the E string on this; it dies after second position."

And while it's common to take a used car to a mechanic or two for an opinion, Waddle says evaluating instruments from other shops makes many makers uncomfortable. "It really bothers me when somebody takes an instrument out on trial from my shop and brings it to another shop for their opinion—like they're going to get an objective opinion from the other shop. And if people call me and they've got a violin from another shop, my feeling is, why are they asking me? If they don't trust the other person, why would they want to buy from them?"

MAKING THE FINAL DECISION

Once you've been to a shop and have narrowed the selection to one or two instruments, it's standard procedure to take it out for a week, try it at home, take it to a lesson, and take it to orchestra rehearsal. You need to try it in all the situations in which you play. You should also remember that instruments might not sound their best until you've played them for a half hour. "If an instrument has some essence or quality that you like, give it some time," Givens says, "because you need to play a lot of instruments for half an hour before they warm up, before the colors and the responsiveness really show themselves."

Givens also emphasizes the importance of buying an instrument in good condition. Otherwise two years may pass and old repairs will fail, old cracks will develop into something more serious, or the neck will collapse. All of a sudden, your instrument has to go in for a major restoration that costs thousands of dollars—and it comes out sounding and feeling much different from what you remembered and loved. That's a heartbreaker, Givens says. So do business with places that are concerned about condition and can offer follow-up support and care.

In addition, do business with a shop that offers future trading or selling options. Most places will give 100 percent trade minus any kind of repair necessary to put the instrument into saleable condition. Also, find out if the company you bought the instrument from will put it on the market for you if you don't need it anymore. Some always will, and some never will, Givens says.

Above all, the thing to remember about buying that first nice instrument is that you're the one who needs to be happy with it because you're the one who is going to be playing it. There are many audiences to consider, but the most important audience is yourself. The sound that instrument makes under your ear must be pleasing. Trust your own judgment about its responsiveness, its voice.

"When you practice, you want a sound that's really inspiring and satisfying," Givens says. "I feel that way about my cello. When I sit down to play, regardless of how much time I've had to practice, I want that sound to be glorious."

FINDING AN AFFORDABLE ANTIQUE INSTRUMENT

by James N. McKean

Auction reports, like Hollywood gossip columns, tend to focus their attention on the stars. The news is of the records, the highest prices, the most ever paid for this or that maker, whether dead or (once in a blue moon) still living. While of some interest, such a perspective tends to be a disservice to the average musician; it leads him or her to believe that it takes a lifetime of debt to get a decent violin and anything less represents a serious compromise in quality.

Nothing could be further from the truth. Granted, unlimited funds can get you a great fiddle (although they don't guarantee it). But, believe it or not, there is life in the antique violin market below six figures. Perhaps more incredible, true excellence is to be found for less money than you might expect to spend for a Honda.

The trick is to establish your priorities before you begin looking. That might sound rather obvious, but the sad truth is that too many people begin on the wrong foot: they figure out the most they can afford to spend and then try only instruments that fall in that narrow bracket. After getting discouraged, they decide to broaden the search—to a higher price range.

Usually they would be better off going in the opposite direction. How so? The answer is simple: the price of a violin has very little to do with the way it sounds. From a commercial point of view, violins are a part of the antique market, and the way they are valued is governed by the same rules. Whether it is for furniture, snuffboxes, rare pictures, or violins, what is of paramount importance is provenance and purity. That's fine, if what you're interested in is antiques. But if what you need is a tool to do your job, or just to make music, then the amount you spend does not necessarily reflect what you get.

The hierarchy of the violin world is set in general terms—a maker's perceived worth is determined largely by where and when he worked. (Unfortunately, we

This Ernst Heinrich Roth violin, built in the late 1940s, was purchased by an amateur player for less than $5,000.

know of only one or two women violin makers active before the middle of this century.) Thus we find that the works of a second-rate maker who happened to be an Italian working in the 18th century fetch much higher prices than those of the best Berlin copyists of the early 20th century, even though the latter often are tonally superior and much more suited to the way

What you need is not a name but a violin that was made by an experienced, well-trained maker.

music is made today. It's no secret that there are instruments by the very top makers that are dogs but that nevertheless command hundreds of thousands of dollars. Is it because they still sound so much better than the best works of less celebrated makers? Hardly.

This strange state of affairs can work to your advantage if you have a clear idea of what you need in a violin. Most musicians today require projection, power, and quality. So do you really need a Testore, Rocco, Vuillaume, Postacchini, or Cuypers? No. The audience can't read the label (which is probably a facsimile anyway), and the audition committee can't even see what it is you are playing. There are plenty of top instruments available in the antique market, but what you need is not a name but a violin that was made by an experienced, well-trained maker who used the Strad or Guarneri model and the finest wood, with a top-quality varnish, a well-executed arch, good graduations, and a condition as close to mint as you can find. These are the factors that make a good-sounding instrument that will give you a lifetime of dependable service.

Looked at from this point of view, there is a plenitude of instruments in the lower range ($50,000 and less). That kind of money gets you into the lower end of the older Italians (which means, basically, a dead 19th- or 20th-century maker), and they're nothing to write home about. To understand why, we need to look back at the factors that produce a suitable sound for today's player.

At the top of the list of ingredients for a good sound is the model, the Stradivari or Guarneri del Gesù. In the 18th century, both of these makers were radicals, which is reflected in the fact that violins by Stradivari only came into their own during the 1790s, when Giovanni Battista Viotti began using one; as for del Gesù, it was in the early 19th century, when Niccolò Paganini began playing on one after he lost his Strad in a card game, as the story goes. By that time, the Golden Age of Italian making (1575–1784) was long dead, and Stradavari and del Gesù were back to doing what had always worked so well: using the patterns of Stainer and Amati.

Both are beautiful designs, perfect for producing a certain type of sound. But there is a very good reason why makers eventually stopped using them: they were increasingly unsuited to the changing world of the concert musician, who needed, among other things, greater projection. However, these are the instruments you will be seeing if you move into this low to middle price range of Italian instruments. A violin doesn't have to be a slavish imitation of the work of either Strad or del Gesù, but the chances are that if it has been made with a good understanding of the acoustic properties of these models, it will sound good.

Now figure out what factors drive up the prices of instruments. As mentioned before, primary among these is provenance. A "School of Rocca" violin sells for a fraction of what the genuine article does. What the violin itself sounds like is not a factor in this relative pricing; it is entirely a matter of whether the experts agree that it was made by Rocca's hand. However, if you have set sound as your own primary consideration, the fact of whether or not it was his work is not important, and you are in a position to get a violin that suits your needs for a much more affordable cost. If the violin is "possibly Italian" or is what is enigmatically referred to as "an interesting violin," then the price is even lower. All the better; if it sounds good and its condition is sound, you are getting all you need without paying a surcharge for considerations that don't matter to you.

INVESTMENT VALUE AND ANTIQUE VIOLINS

Many people are concerned, in this situation, with the investment value of what they are getting. It is true that instruments without a pedigree do not go up in value as fast as those by established makers. But, again, look at your criteria; is "an investment" on the list? It shouldn't be; in selecting a violin, you should be thinking solely of the job you need it for—to make music.

If you do buy a violin as an investment, then you should recognized that you are entering the art market, and any investment advisor will tell you what that entails: speculation, and therefore risk. The tremendous boom in the art market in the 1980s misled many people into believing that buying art is a good way to get rich. In reality, study after study has shown that art, in terms of real growth over the long term, does relatively poorly—and this is still true even when the boom of the '80s is figured in. Much of the fantastic price gain during that period was in a very narrow field, that of French Impressionist paintings. If someone tells you violins are a fabulous investment, he or she is being disingenuous. While the art market has shown real growth over the past century, it has been consistently outpaced by the stock market—and this is without factoring in the extra costs you face with violins, such as insurance, conservation, and interest on any loan you may have taken out.

There is also the matter of wear and tear; one of the many components of value in the antique market is purity, and playing a violin hours a day for decades is hardly a good way to protect that part of the investment. Most people with rare instruments end up buying inexpensive ones to use as their workhorses. You can make money investing in fiddles, but it is far from guaranteed, and it requires a fairly sophisticated knowledge of what is, in truth, an obscure corner of the art market.

If you weren't a violinist, would you be buying an antique violin as one of your primary vehicles for savings?

Think of it this way: if you weren't a violinist, would you be buying an antique violin as one of your primary vehicles for savings? It might be instructive to take a look at the rest of the orchestra, outside of the string section. They all play instruments and get paid the same as you do. Chances are excellent that many of them are doing a very good job of investing their money, and that none of them feel the need to include a rare Italian violin in their portfolio. If violins are such a great investment, then why don't more nonviolinists buy them? In some ways, a violin without a pedigree but with a good sound is not at all a bad investment; musicians will always want it, and its value is not dependent on the opinions of experts, with which time often has a way of playing tricks.

THE NATIONALITY FACTOR

In addition to provenance, a key factor that drives up the price of instruments is nationality. Italian works command a premium; next are French, Dutch or English, then German instruments, and then—barely within spitting distance—American. In general, one might argue that these categorizations have some validity, but there are enough good and bad violins in each school to mean that many instruments suffer or benefit unfairly from this preconception. If your primary concern is a good sound, then you can stand aside and let others pay extra for their prejudices. The influence of Stradivari and del Gesù did not become dominant until the 19th century, and by this time one finds very accomplished makers in every country.

German instruments and bows have always been stigmatized as having a faint whiff of the factory about them, and it is true that Germany supplied the world with most of its entry-level instruments (and, considering what they were sold for and

A Bohemian violin, by Joannes Helmer (Prague, 1755). This instrument, in immediate playing condition, sold for only $4,600.

whom they were intended for, they were an excellent product). However, there were many makers in Germany who produced top-quality instruments, and one will rarely find them priced for much more than $30,000—and usually for much less.

One of the first to adopt the Stradivari model was Franz Geissenhof. Here we run into another common prejudice, which is to lump everyone east of Alsace into a generic pile called "German." There were myriad schools active in the territory of the German states and the Austro-Hungarian empire from the 17th century on (and even earlier; Füssen, in southern Germany, is now accepted as the source of many of the early luthiers, even those who later turned up in Italy). Geissenhof was in fact a Viennese maker; other notable makers of that city were Johann Martin Stoss and Gabriel Lemböck, who was reputed to have obtained his del Gesù patterns from Paganini's own violin when it was brought to him for repair. Another good maker was Andreas Carl Leeb, whose cellos are particularly fine. He employed a device that, sadly, has fallen out of use, a key like that used to wind a clock that could be inserted into the heel of the cello neck to adjust the height of the strings.

The prices are ridiculously low for the quality you can find in a violin that has no specific maker and gets called a "Bohemian violin" or "of the Czech school." These may be had for less than $10,000. Many musicians have heard of Samuel Nemessányi, usually as a copyist whose fakes can fool the experts. They can't, but his reputation has caused a run-up in the prices for his instruments (of which there are very few—so be careful if you are offered one). One of his assistants was Béla Szepessy, whose instruments are also quite good. They turn up frequently at auction, for he eventually established himself in London. A fellow assistant to Nemessányi whose work is spoken of quite highly was Carl Hermann Voigt. Budapest had other makers whose work was very respectable, among them Thomas Zach and his assistant, J.B. Schweitzer (although one must exercise caution with the later; his own work varied, and after he died a lot of truly cheap violins were stamped with his name). The Boston Symphony Orchestra at one point was outfitted with a complete set of instruments made by Thomas Zach's son Karl. Prague also had several makers in the 19th century who worked off the Strad model with great success. Some of the best were J.B. Dvořák, along with Caspar Strand and his assistant Ferdinand Homolka.

Many people associate the name Roth with cheap factory-style work. But, the reality is more complicated. Ernst Heinrich Roth himself was a first-class maker, although one rarely comes across instruments made entirely by him. In addition, he established a commercial operation that became quite large, exporting instruments around the world and particularly to America. These instruments range in quality

This 1882 violin was made by August Gemunder, one American maker worth seeking out for reliable, low-cost antique violins.

from basic student models to works that are quite respectable, particularly those from the 1920s and '30s that were billed as the top of the line. These instruments can be beautiful copies based on Strad or del Gesù models. With some work (usually less than it takes to get the average modern Italian sounding decent), they can be made to sound quite good. The top-of-the-line instruments sell at around $6,000. Any dealer can tell you that prospective purchasers are astonished when they play some of these instruments. Their good sound, however, should come as no surprise—after all, they were made by master makers on acoustically good patterns, with top-quality materials and an excellent oil varnish. Many of my colleagues look at these instruments and say, "What I could have done with that wood!" Which overlooks the fact that what was done with the wood was actually first-rate.

Another name that people often put in the same rank is Neuner-Hornsteiner, a factory that operated from the turn of the century on. However, Ludwig Neuner worked with Vuillaume, and his own work is very respectable. One often comes across instruments from the Heberlein shop, which was another large commercial concern; the violins of H.T. Heberlein are quite good, similar to the best made by Roth.

Karl Grimm was a copyist whom experts agree was one of the very best—one of the few, in fact, whose works have passed as originals. He worked in Berlin in the early 19th century. Another excellent maker was his assistant, Oswald Möckel, whose son Otto was highly respected in the 20th century. His copies of Stradivari, Guadagnini, and del Gesù are wonderful violins. It is a shame that the works of these makers are so little known, although it works to your advantage if you find one, for the prices are much lower than what one would expect for instruments of this quality. I would even disregard my own comments about stringed instruments as a financial investment when it comes to this school—they are woefully underpriced (which I can say objectively, for I'm sad to say I don't own a single one). It should not be surprising that Berlin had outstanding makers; by the late 19th century, it had become one of the centers of the violin world, boasting of stars such as Pablo de Saraste and Joseph Joachim.

There has been much discussion in recent years about American violins, and there are excellent instruments to be found, although the general level of achievement is lower than that of other national schools. For the most part, the makers fall into two categories, European émigré or self-taught. The former were almost all from Germany, and they were found mainly in Chicago, Philadelphia, Boston, and New York. Many of them established large shops, with the result that works by their own hand can be rare; but the violins from their shops are usually of a very high standard. Charles Albert, in Philadelphia, was one of the best known, along with

John Hornsteiner of Chicago. The latter had learned the trade from Matthias Neuner in Berlin, who, as we saw earlier, worked with Vuillaume. Many of Hornsteiner's violins were actually made by his assistant Frank Sindelar, who went on his own in 1917, operating a shop in Chicago until the end of the Second World War. Another pupil of Hornsteiner was Carl Becker, Sr., also of Chicago.

New York was home to several large shops, the most notable being that of the Gemunder brothers, August and George, who, after a brief partnership, worked separately. Their instruments are worth seeking out. George Gemunder had worked for J.B. Vuillaume in Paris, and he made instruments in that style but with his own distinctive character. As did other shops, such as that of John Friedrich and H.R. Knopf (both also of New York), the Gemunders sold a line of shop violins of varying levels of refinement; they can be quite respectable and are still valued at a very low cost.

American-born and -trained makers of a professional level were few and far between, but that can work to your advantage—the prices of their works are held down by the general perception that there were none worth talking about. The Conn Wonder Violin was the product of a huge operation, rivaling in scope the mass production facilities of Germany. It was begun in the 19th century by an ex-Union soldier, C.G. Conn, and while most of the fiddles were of that same level of quality—which is still quite professional—the business also employed three makers who signed their own violins and whose works are of the first rank. Ironically, the best of these was of Italian descent, William Pezzoni, from Brooklyn. His violins are much superior to many of the modern Italian makers and, if you can find any, sell at a fraction of the cost. Margaret Downie Banks wrote a thorough piece on Conn in the *Violin Society Journal* (Vol. 11, No. 3, November 1990).

A man who was perhaps the best known of the native-trained American violin makers was J.B. Squier (unlike the initials of so many of his colleagues, the J.B. doesn't stand for Jean Baptiste; instead it's Jerome Bonapart). His background was in the colorful tradition of John Lott, the celebrated English elephant trainer and del Gesù copyist. Squier began as a farmer in Michigan, then was a shoemaker and, as far as violin making goes, was essentially self-taught. He moved to Boston in 1881 and produced a large number of instruments, working with his adopted son Victor Carroll, and they can be quite nice. They are found at around $8,000. J.B. Squier is described as having devoted the greater part of his time to varnish experiments; in this, one could say that American violin making has changed very little in the intervening century.

There were many more of these makers across the country; an invaluable guide to them is the comprehensive *Violin Makers of the United States* by Thomas James Wenberg (Mt. Hood Publishing, 1986). Skinner, the Boston auction house, is a good source for American instruments, since they turn up there regularly—so you can find one at a great price before it heads to Europe, where chances are excellent that the label will be pulled and it will be sold as a modern Italian.

Good luck in your search; it is well worth the effort to get to know some of these unsung Cinderellas. When you find one, and other musicians ask you what you play (no one else will, because no one else cares), you can tell them that you play the violin. And then tell them about the house you got with the money you didn't spend on a fancy label.

CHOOSING A CONTEMPORARY INSTRUMENT

by Wendy Moes

Why are new instruments drawing so much attention? Perhaps people are making better ones. Or perhaps the world's string-playing population is outgrowing its supply of able-bodied old instruments. Or the prices of these antiques are getting too high. Or all of the above. Whatever the reasons, the stigma that was once attached to a brand-new stringed instrument seems to be less and less evident. Today, renowned players are recognizing the worthiness of new instruments and using them proudly in public.

This recognition encourages violin makers to invest their time and talents in making instruments to an extent never possible before. Many of these makers have backgrounds in repair and setup. With extensive knowledge of the classical maker's methods, successes, and failures, they are equipped to make real advances in both the quality of sound and the appearance of new instruments.

A common mistake is to assume that any old instrument is better than any new one. People come to us often and say, "I already have a new violin" (as if they were all the same). "I am looking for something better now" (an old one). Some people think that anything Italian is better than anything that is not. This is certainly not true with modern instruments; there are good contemporary makers all over the world. The very best old instruments can beat the new ones, but there is a lot of middle ground. Unless the status of an expensive old instrument is absolutely vital to your career, you could well consider a new instrument. It could have the sound and playability you are looking for. The lack of interest in new instruments on the part of dealers, though unnerving, probably has more to do with low profit margins than low quality of sound. When a maker sells an instrument, dealers are not usually involved—a good reason for their lack of enthusiasm.

Violin Society of America gold medal winner, William Robert Scott, produces contemporary violins of very high quality.

New makers have a distinct advantage over the classical makers: They can build for today's players and today's halls, both enormously changed in the last 50 to 100 years. When players want more focus, quicker response, and a fuller bass sound, they can now ask that such qualities be built into their instruments. In posing such challenges, they set the stage for creativity and ingenuity on the part of makers. Both players and makers then enjoy a new sense of collaboration and of taking a meaningful role in the evolution of instrument playing.

WHAT TO LOOK FOR IN A CONTEMPORARY VIOLIN

When looking for any instrument, the biggest considerations are authenticity, condition, sound quality, and appearance. The harrowing thing about the first two is that both are matters of opinion, and worse yet, usually *someone else's* opinion. And violin dealers seem to make a sport of disagreeing with one another. One of the biggest differences between antique and modern violins is that authenticity and condition are both givens in the case of new instruments. To many people there is also something special about the experience of ordering a new instrument, seeing the rough wood (sometimes even getting to choose it), and watching the instrument grow. This certainly matches the excitement of owning an instrument that has had many experiences you have not shared.

Sound quality is still the major factor in choosing an instrument, new or old. So a little preparation is necessary in order to learn what sound you like best. Before you spend time and money looking for the right violin, play every instrument you can get your hands on, borrowing them from friends, teachers, and stand partners. Play each one at length—for hours, not minutes. Chances are great that the technique you use on your present instrument won't be an instant success on others. This does not make them bad instruments. Try changing the bow speed, pressure, and sounding points. Play on different kinds of strings. You will get used to changing instruments and finding out how each responds. Discuss the pros and cons of each with their owners and other players. This is very good for opening your eyes and ears, and it will help you develop your opinion of what good sound is and what suits you best.

This vital knowledge applies to new and old instruments alike. With new instruments, one question that often arises is whether the sound will change. This is an age-old problem with improperly built instruments, and it deserves some demystification.

This violin by Joseph Curtin was built in 1998 but is fashioned after a Guarneri model.

Everybody knows a young branch will bend and an old one will snap. This stiffening process goes on long after the tree has been cut. A stiff piece of wood vibrates differently than a flexible one, resulting in a higher and more complete overtone series. We can't hear all the overtones, but we perceive the sound to be more full and pleasant. This means a well-made instrument will improve with age as it stiffens, but it should sound good to begin with. A bad-sounding instrument will not necessarily get better and could get worse.

Proper arching and graduations are also necessary. An instrument built to be too thick or strong will gradually get too stiff to vibrate freely. Be cautious about an instrument that feels heavy, and about sound quality that is quite good on the top string but fades toward the bottom string. The lower register requires more flexibility and suffers first when the instrument begins to stiffen.

The other factors that can cause New Instrument Syndrome ("It sounded great to begin with, but now . . . ") are improper sizing and varnish. Watch out for thick varnish and varnish that soaks into the wood. This is often the case when the wood looks stained and the grain is reversed. Such instruments can sound fine for a while, until the varnish begins to harden and hamper the vibrations. A knowledgeable maker can avoid these problems. The violin maker, like a painter, must know his or her materials, how they age, and how they affect each other.

If you have a particular maker in mind, play as many of his or her already existing instruments as possible. Play those that are as old as possible to see and hear what age does to them. Discuss sound and changes, if any, with the present owner. When you find a maker whose instruments you like, consider whether he or she is easily accessible. This is important because a new instrument needs extra service for the first year or so. After vibrating and being under tension for a while, a new instrument can settle, as can an older instrument that has been opened for repair work. This settling usually takes the form of soundpost tension (see "What Do the

Bass Bar and Soundpost Do?," page 23) and changes in the neck angle (see "The Proper Neck Angle," page 77). Be prepared to make several trips to the maker during that first year. If settling problems go unadjusted, the instrument could appear to change or lose some of its sound quality.

ESTABLISHING A RAPPORT WITH YOUR VIOLIN MAKER

It very often happens that players with new instruments from other makers come to us for adjustments, saying, "He makes fine instruments, but he cannot adjust for beans." Some players and makers are almost proud of this, as if it proves the makers are artists and not mere mechanics. To us, it means the maker doesn't have a full understanding of how instruments work. Violins, unlike art, must not only look appealing but also function very precisely. Understanding how they work and how to make them work is absolutely essential and comes before artistry. The maker's artistic merit will show up automatically in the amount of personality and character he or she puts into the work.

Until recently, a great number of musicians were reluctant to play any instrument that looked new. But that prejudice is rapidly disappearing. The instruments of Stradivari, Amati, and Guarneri were all once new. They looked it, and they looked great—fit for kings. They were not antiqued. It is not the newness of some modern instruments that makes them unsightly, and it is not the age alone of old instruments that lends them their charm. The charm was there to begin with in the character of the work and the varnish, and it should be there in new instruments, too.

Audiences, by the way, are notoriously unable to hear the differences between old and new instruments. Any soloist who owns a new instrument—and there are many now who do—can tell stories by the dozen of green-room compliments on the Stradivari or Guarneri, when the performer had actually played the new one that night. The best instrument is the one that performs and handles best for the player, not the one with the biggest price tag or the most venerable reputation. When you next look for an instrument, keep that fact in mind. You may end up living happily ever after with something brand new.

SELECTING A BOW

by Susan M. Barbieri

The French term for the bow is *baguette,* which is fitting, since a good bow comple-ments an instrument like a thick slice of fresh bread complements a gourmet meal. People spend so much time trying to find the right violin, viola, or cello that they often give short shrift to its better half. So after you've chosen your first good instru-ment (see "Considering Your First Good Instrument," page 29), you should repeat the winnowing process for the bow.

Don't try to shop for an instrument and a bow at the same time, or you'll drive yourself nuts. The process is complicated enough when you're simply trying to choose an instrument. If you add the separate winnowing process for choosing a bow, you run the risk of hopelessly confusing yourself and deadening your ears to the subtleties of a given stick. It's better to break down the instrument- and bow-shopping process into two stages: first look for the instrument, then for the bow that suits both it and you.

Lydia Rose, a Minnesota bow maker and cellist, says it is just as important to look carefully for the bow as it is to find the perfect instrument. Like instruments, no two bows are alike. "They're much more unique than instruments are," says Rose, who studied bow making in Belgium with a French maker. "I'll hear people play on the same instrument with the same bow, and the bow will sound quite dif-ferent in each person's hands. You have to go by how you feel, and your teacher can help you a lot."

If you're looking at a $2,000–$4,000 violin, you should be looking at a bow that costs at least $500, she says. And based on her experience working in violin shops and watching people test instruments and bows, she finds that for $250 or $500 more in a bow, you can make your instrument sound $1,000 better. The money actually goes a lot further in a bow than it does in an instrument, Rose contends.

WHERE TO BEGIN

Midwestern bow maker Roger Zabinski says the first and most overwhelming consideration in selecting a bow is sound. And although opinion is greatly divided on this point, Zabinski advises people not to buy something solely for the sake of investment. "Don't think about how much you're going to be able to get out of it when you sell it," he says. "It's not an investment; it's a musical instrument."

When you're buying a bow made by an individual craftsman, you may want to find out if the maker has entered competitions and how well they've done. This can help you establish some sense of reputation and determine the quality of the person's work. Then get a feeling for the draw of the bow from frog to tip. "How does it

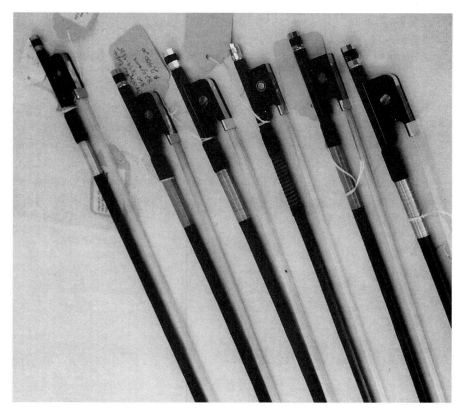

Selecting a bow is a difficult endeavor, and making a checklist can help. Evaluate each bow for strength, balance, playability, aesthetics, and price.

feel end to end, just on an open string?" asks Zabinski. "Is the sound connected end to end or does it change and make you have to change pressure and speed to maintain the same kind of sound? How does it draw?"

Look for a bow of moderate strength and flexibility. With very strong bows, you lose a lot in sound quality and nuance. And with one that's too soft, you lose control. If you're torn between one that's light and one that's a bit heavier, go for the lighter one, Zabinski says. You'll get clearer trebles, more delicacy.

Remember that it takes at least a day to get adjusted to the feel of a different bow. A player will tend to gravitate toward a bow that feels like the old one, even though the old one is probably of lower quality. Typically, the fiberglass or cheap wooden bow a student has been using has poor balance and is not lively in the hand. (A step up would be a bow of either brazilwood or pernambuco; of those, pernambuco is the higher-grade wood.) Trying a more responsive bow can be unsettling. "If you get one of these bows that has really nice balance, it can feel light, and if it's really lively, it can feel like it's going all over the strings, because you're used to working so hard to get the bow to go, and all of a sudden it just springs," Rose says.

"When you're looking for a bow, there are several characteristics that change how it feels in your hand," Rose continues. "The first one is weight. For a violin bow, the optimal weight is between 60 and 65 grams, although 65 is really heavy. For a viola bow, it's between 70 and 73. A cello bow is about 80 and up, and often cellists in the U.S. tend to like them over 80; 82 or 83 is a common weight for a cello bow.

"Another characteristic has to do with the way the bow digs into the strings. You want a bow that will dig in without the wood hitting the string. If you're digging, you can get that nice accented sound. But if the bow isn't strong enough, the stick will flex so much that the hair is caught between the string and the bow and you don't have as much control over it."

Elasticity is another important characteristic, but it's a tougher concept to understand. A musician might describe a bow lacking elasticity as "sluggish" or "unresponsive." The quality of the wood determines its elasticity.

Rose remembers when she got her first decent cello bow. Looking back now from the vantage point of a bow maker, she is surprised at the quality of the wood in that stick.

"If you get this kind of pernambuco that's really high quality, you can actually feel the vibrations of the string as they travel all the way down the stick. The difference between brazilwood and pernambuco, and I'm talking a really good piece of brazilwood and a really good piece of pernambuco, is that the brazilwood has the strength and the weight, but it doesn't have the elasticity that the pernambuco has."

The characteristic that may be most critical is the balance. A lot of bows that are $750 or under lack balance and tend to be rather tip-heavy, Rose says. A player counteracting that gets tired sooner.

She advises paying attention to the aesthetics of the bow as well—the workmanship, the camber of the stick. And, naturally, condition is important when shopping for bows, especially if you are choosing an old one. A bow that has been broken at the head and repaired is never a good buy because it may come apart again. A repair at the frog is less important, though you shouldn't pay too high a price for such a bow. As when buying your instrument, you'll want to make sure you purchase your bow from a shop that will maintain it after the sale. It's not unusual for bows to warp, for example, but that's an easy problem for a good maker to fix. And you'll want to know the shop's trade-in policy, for the day you decide to move up to a bow of yet higher quality.

Because it can be so overwhelming to shop for bows, Rose suggests making a checklist (it's a trick that helps when you're shopping for an instrument, too). Write the bows down on one side and make columns across the top with characteristics: strength, balance, how well it plays staccato and spiccato.

"When you're trying out bows, try doing really long détaché bows," she advises. "Just play some long scales to see how even it feels. Then try doing spiccato passages. Play a scale and do 16th-note staccato so you can feel how it balances. Do some martelé. Then play some pieces to see how comfortable it feels in your hand. Try playing softly and loudly."

NARROWING DOWN YOUR CHOICES

There is a standard, two-step process that can help players choose a bow. First, concentrate on judging just the bow's sound, then consider the response. Choose four or five bows and play each one against the other, and just listen to the sound. Don't even think about the handling or response; just concentrate on the sound you are producing. Go back and fourth between your test bows until you have narrowed your choices down to two.

Once you've narrowed down your choices, test your favorites to see how they respond. Play pieces that require different bow strokes. Be sure to test all dynamic levels and play at both the tip and the frog, taking both long and short notes.

Zabinski has a few "don'ts" for players shopping for their first good bow. For one, don't pay too much attention to how quickly it dances off the strings; the very greatest bows have rather soft spiccatos. "It's a bad test," he says. "That's on the bottom of the list. Yes, you do have to be able to get off the string, but when you're making music almost all of your music is melody, where you want long, drawn bows and you're just simply making sound. These fancy, splashy things are a very small part of music making and aren't a particularly accurate measure of bow quality."

Secondly, Zabinski adds, "don't necessarily be beguiled by silvery, satiny-smooth sounds. The best bows have a little bit of reediness to them, not a hard edge, but a little bit of a reedy edge that creates a color and texture that carries, that the listener perceives as classy and noble." He adds that it's a good idea to ask your teacher and others who are musically close to you to listen as you play the bow. Even parents who insist that they don't know anything about music often come up with astute observations about the sound of one bow versus another when they listen to their child play. The key, of course, is that you must be the one playing; the bow will sound completely different in someone else's hands.

Finally, avoid glitzy-looking bows. You pay a lot for glitz and may not get much substance, says Zabinski. Simply buy the highest quality of bow you can buy. "It's the bow that will really assist or hinder a student's development," he says, "much more than the instrument itself. It's more important to buy as much of a bow as you can. In fact, oftentimes one can significantly upgrade one's sound and ability just by buying a better bow. It's breathtaking what a bow can do."

CHOOSING A CASE

by Heather K. Scott

Shopping for a violin case can be a daunting task. Your options range from basic cases that list for under $300 to truly beautiful pieces of art costing thousands of dollars. In deciding which instrument case is right for you, consider your lifestyle, your environment, and your budget. Make use of the Internet, which provides a unique opportunity to do some preliminary research and window shopping. It also helps to make a list of what you are looking for, what you can afford, and preferred companies *before* you venture out to your local music store.

There are many violin cases to choose from, ranging from basic options that list for under $300 to truly beautiful pieces of art that cost thousands of dollars.

The interior of a Musafia Master's Series case.

What type of case will best suit your needs? Because of their durability, hard-shell cases tend to be more popular with musicians looking for assurance that their instruments will be protected. Their traditional disadvantage has been a tendency to be very heavy. But these days there are more and more lightweight cases on the market that are designed to hold your instrument tightly in place and provide a good deal of protection. If you're content with your current case and only wish it were easier to carry around, you might want to look at case bags, which provide additional padding and make heavy cases more manageable via comfortable handles and backpack straps.

Contemporary cases offer a plethora of options. The five-star-hotel equivalents will pamper and spoil any instrument, but not everyone needs a luxury case. You should be aware, however, of the practical amenities that address basic care and maintenance concerns. Changes in temperature and humidity can wreak havoc on your instrument, so if you live in an area with an extreme climate, consider adding a hygrometer and a humidifier to your case wish list. Hygrometers measure humidity levels, letting you know if your instrument is too damp or too dry; humidifiers correct dryness (a common problem, especially in winter), usually via a small tube filled with water-saturated material that releases moisture at a controlled rate. If a hygrometer and humidifier are the case features you are most concerned about—and if you are looking for the most accurate equipment—you might be best off buying a stripped-down case and installing a hygrometer and humidifier yourself (you may also look into have a shop do this for you). You can purchase specific hygrometers and humidifiers to fit your needs through most music shops and distributors.

Think about how many interior and exterior compartments you need. Will you be traveling with a portfolio case? Sheet music? Cases generally have between one and four inner compartments and one outer sheet-music compartment running the length of the case. Some include gusseted outer pockets for extra storage and others feature a detachable exterior pocket for carrying portfolios. Do you have several bows? Some cases have only one or two bow holders, some four. And even if you have only one bow, be sure to bring it to the store to make sure that it fits in the holder provided.

Investigate your potential case thoroughly. Look at everything from the instrument padding or suspension system to the hardware. Suspension cases have become the norm for most companies and are almost always preferable. They are well padded and prevent your instrument from resting flat against the bottom of the case, which can be dangerous if the case receives a blow or is dropped. The instrument neck is held in place with a Velcro flap or string tie, and padding hugs the instrument tightly in place. Keeping an instrument safe while traveling is an overwhelming concern for most instrumentalists. While most cases will fit in overhead compartments on airplanes, airlines' ever-tightening carry-on limitations increase the possibility of being forced to check your instrument—so the harder the outer case and the softer the suspension system, the better.

Most cases also include a zipper-and-lock system. For security, look for two zippers that start in the back and meet at the center front. Some of the better cases have weather flaps that shelter the zippers and Velcro or snaps encasing the vulnerable spot where the zippers meet. Zippered cases may or may not lock, but those without zippers generally do. Sometimes one lock at the center of the case below the handle is the only way to secure the case. Sometimes two or even three locks are mounted along the sides of the case, with an additional snap-down weather flap to cover the hardware.

I spoke with several professional, touring musicians at the San Francisco Symphony to learn what they look for when shopping for instrument cases. Many pros sacrifice comfort for durability and depend more on sturdy designs than aesthetically pleasing ones. Geraldine Walther, the symphony's principal violist, uses a Weber case. "A suspension system was the most important thing I looked for," she told me. "Bow holders were important too, but I really just wanted it to feel sturdy. I also needed it to fit a narrow viola, because I have a 16¡. The Weber is pretty heavy, but it's sturdy."

The real challenge is to find a case that's nearly bulletproof but also feels comfortable when carried long distances. Assistant Concertmaster Jeremy Constant found himself in a situation no musician anticipates. "We were on tour in New York and something got spilled in my violin case, so I needed a new case very, very quickly," he recalled. "I was looking for suspension construction and a hard shell. My feeling was that soft cases did not offer enough protection for me."

Constant purchased a Musafia case partly for the long, wick-style humidifier it features. "When you are touring in the winter, it is a godsend," he explained, "because everything is so horrifically dry. Dampits [sponge-like humidifiers] are a losing effort unless you are willing to have one in each f-hole." The Musafia is expensive, Constant admitted, but for him it was well worth the investment.

Even the most expensive case can't protect your instrument from more than 30 minutes of extreme temperatures. And, no matter how advanced your case humidifier is, you should still maintain optimal humidity levels in the place in which you store your instrument. A hygrometer and humidifier will help you measure and maintain these levels. Dial-reading hygrometers tend to be less accurate than digital hygrometers (look for the Stretto, available in the UK from Frederick Phelps Ltd, 67 Fortass Road, Kentish Town, London NW5 1AG. Tel: 0207 4820316. www.phelps-violins.com). Digital equipment may provide the most accurate temperature and humidity measurement and control, functioning up to two weeks compared with the two-day duration of most other humidification systems.

When shopping for an instrument case, look around, compare prices, and try out as many cases as possible. You generally do get what you pay for (especially when it comes to hardware and other materials), but remember that you may not need all the extras. You can get a reasonable amount of protection at a reasonable price. Whether your main concern is the winter dryness cracking your instrument's varnish or surviving a trip to rehearsals on an uncomfortably packed city bus, there are many cases to fit your needs.

WHEN IT'S TIME
TO SELL YOUR
INSTRUMENT

by Jana Luckey

Selling an instrument can arouse all kinds of conflicting emotions. You, and perhaps also your family, probably put a lot of thought into buying it. It was an important financial commitment at the time, and it represented an investment in your continued progress. You and that instrument have been through a lot together. But while there may very well be a part of you that wants to make sure it goes to a good home, it's still time to move on. You're head over heels in love—with another instrument.

If you sell your instrument directly to retail, you can avoid involving a dealer.

Even in matters of love, however, there are times when it is critical to think clearly. When selling an instrument, you need to get in touch with that cold, hard place deep inside that can be ruthless, calculating, and shrewd. You need to be able to put yourself in the place of the buyer, whether you're considering selling the instrument on your own, working with an auction house, or approaching a dealer or the instrument's maker. It takes some research to determine the current market value of the instrument you want to sell, but it pays to educate yourself before putting it on the market.

PROVENANCE AND CONDITION: WHAT MAKES THE SALE

For stringed instruments, provenance and condition will govern the price you can reasonably ask. This is one of many reasons why you must always be sure, back at the stage when you're buying the instrument, that you are purchasing from a reputable, competent source. Provenance is the consensus of expert opinion as to the authorship of your instrument. If you own a contemporary instrument or a commercial one (made mostly by machine in a workshop or factory), you probably know its provenance. If, on the other hand, you have an older instrument, you may have documents such as a certificate of authenticity or an insurance appraisal that will attribute the instrument to a particular maker or school. The more reliable and specific the attribution and the more attractive that provenance is to the current market, the more your instrument will be worth.

Condition will influence the value of any kind of instrument. If your instrument has not required extensive restoration work and it's been maintained regularly by a reputable repairer, you shouldn't have much to worry about when it comes time to sell. If, however, you bought the instrument and subsequently found out that some of its repairs were not well done, you could have a problem on your hands. One professional violinist resolved this sticky situation by trading in her instrument when she found a stunning Italian violin she wanted to buy at a dealer's. "I had recently been told by a repairperson I trust that there had been some poor work done on my old fiddle. I didn't want to sell it on my own because I didn't want to have to represent it to potential buyers as being in the best condition."

How provenance and condition contribute to market value is something many instrument owners learn only when they decide to sell. The value of a commercial or trade instrument in good condition may keep pace with new instruments in its class, but it will never have real investment potential. Likewise, the value of an older instrument with a quirky design or poor repair work will see limited appreciation. Players who buy instruments because they like the sound will discover when they try to sell them that tone quality is a factor too subjective to influence market value.

RESEARCH YOUR VIOLIN BEFORE HITTING THE MARKET

Insurance appraisals, regularly updated by a reputable shop, can be a general source of information. James McKean, a New York maker and restorer, notes that appraisals "tend to be on the high side by as much as ten percent, because a dealer will figure in the cost of the time and expense of replacing the instrument." On the other hand, the shop where you bought your instrument may make conservative estimations if its policy is to give you the appraised value as a trade-in toward your next instrument. And appraisals will vary from dealer to dealer, since evaluating the market for a particular instrument is, after all, a subjective business. Still, they are a good starting point.

You should also research the selling price of other instruments like yours. Many dealers now have detailed Internet sites that list what they have available. Maestronet (www.maestronet.com) provides links to many dealers and makers and also offers a centralized listing of instruments for sale through their clients at www.maestronet.com/4sale.html. The Web sites of the major auction houses, such as Sotheby's (www.sothebys.com), Bonhams (www.bonhams.com), Phillips

Selling your violin at auction is an alternative to dealing with the retail market.

(www.phillips-auctions.com), Christie's (www.christies.com), and Skinner (www.skinnerinc.com) put catalogs for upcoming sales on-line. Some even provide sales results from recent auctions, as does *Strings'* annual *Musical Instrument Auction Price Guide.*

Once you have learned everything you can about the violin you will be selling, consider your needs. Are you selling the instrument because you want to get out of the market, are you handling the sale for an estate, or are you no longer playing? Or are you selling to stay in the market? Do you need to sell or trade in this instrument quickly in order to buy another one, or are you in a position where a little patience will allow you to maximize your profit from the transaction?

CHOOSING THE BEST METHOD FOR YOUR SALE

There are several ways to sell an instrument. The more you know about them, the easier it will be to choose the one most appropriate for you. You can sell directly to the retail market, without the involvement of any third party such as a dealer. You can work with an auction house that will sell for a commission at one of a few auctions held each year. If the instrument is by a contemporary maker, you can approach that maker to sell it for you. Or you can go to a dealership and try to sell it outright, consign it, or trade it in toward another instrument you will buy there.

Often, selling an instrument yourself at retail is the most appropriate option if you have a commercial instrument. Most student instruments fall into this category. You can start by posting notices on bulletin boards at university music departments, community music schools, symphony offices, or anywhere else in your community where musicians gather. String teachers, whether working privately or in the public schools, can be an excellent networking source when it comes time to sell a student instrument.

Advertising your instrument in newsletters and periodicals read by teachers, students, and performers is another alternative. The Internet has given a new twist to this method of reaching the retail market; several Web sites now offer classified advertising for stringed instruments, including violinandviola.co.uk, musicalchairs.eu.com and musicalinstrumentsales.co.uk. You can also list your instrument on the auction site www.eBay.com. On eBay, potential buyers can limit a search of available instruments to their region, which makes this service an attractive option.

The upside of selling directly to the retail market is that you have complete control over pricing and your clientele. Your expenses are relatively low because you're doing all the work yourself. If you know what you have to offer and can access the market for your instrument, you may be successful. When setting a price for a commercial instrument, don't expect it to have appreciated. If, however, it's been well maintained and is set up reasonably well, you can price it to attract parents and students who will appreciate the fact that the instrument has been broken in and has held up to use.

Dealers and auction houses will generally not even look at commercial instruments because their clientele is not interested in that market segment. There are however some British exceptions, such as Frederick Phelps of Kentish Town, London who offers 100% of the value of your old instrument against the price of a new violin, provided your old instrument is worth £1000 or more. For instruments valued between £200 and £1000 the trade-in value drops to 75%. Bridgewood and Neitzert of Stoke Newington, London will also accept instruments in part-exchange. They may also buy instruments outright, depending on their current inventory, or will offer to sell them for you at a commission, although they are happier to enter in to such arrrangements with violins originating from their own stock.

There are some distinct disadvantages to selling any instrument on your own. Depending on the market, the competition, and the demand for instruments in your area, it can take a long time to find a buyer. There can be some understandable reluctance on the part of potential buyers to invest in a high-end instrument on an "as is" basis, without a dealership standing behind it. If you decide to advertise the instrument outside your immediate area, insurance issues can arise when someone asks to look at the instrument. Says a cellist who has sold instruments on her own and through dealers, "If you're trying to sell an instrument on your own, just the concept of having it go out your door for a two-week trial period is nerve-racking. Sometimes insurance won't cover the instrument during that trial period. If you're working with a dealer who's trustworthy, you feel much more protected."

Selling your instrument at auction is one alternative to dealing with the retail market. Skinner has emerged as the most accessible auction venue for U.S. sellers, although the fine-instrument departments of the large London houses Sotheby's and Christie's have begun holding sales in the U.S. after several years' hiatus. Skinner's Fine Musical Instrument Department, headed by David Bonsey, is located in Boston and offers several sales each year.

The process of working with an auction house begins with an inspection of your instrument. Kerry Keane, head of Christie's musical instrument department, explains that he assesses a market value and sets a presale estimate, which is expressed as a range. "It's a balancing act to come up with a presale estimate that's defendable," he says. "I'm against putting instruments in a sale if I think there has been overestimation of the value. I saw a Gagliano once whose owner wanted more than $200,000. I didn't think I could defend that price, so I turned it down." He and the consignor then establish a reserve, which is the lowest sale price the consignor will accept. The reserve rests somewhere between two-thirds of the low estimate and the low estimate itself. The lower the reserve, the more likely it is that the item will sell. When Keane and the consignor are in agreement about these figures, they sign a contract and the item is catalogued for the next sale. A contract must be signed no later than 12 weeks before the sale. In addition to the expense of shipping the instrument for inspection, there are also commission and insurance costs involved with auctioning an instrument, which can vary slightly from one auction house to another.

Keane adds that selling an instrument at auction can be the best solution when fiduciaries are trying to settle an estate: "Auction facilitates an expedient sale, casting a wider net to the buying public."

This contrasts with the view of Philip Kass, of William Moennig & Son, Ltd., a Philadelphia dealership. He views auction houses as a last resort for a seller because "at auction, the instrument probably won't fetch top dollar. If it doesn't sell, the instrument has been exposed worldwide at a certain price level, and it will carry a stigma if the seller attempts to offer it again."

Another difficulty involved in working with an auction house is that the seller loses access to the instrument once a contract is signed. Keane concedes that the majority of players he sees have a second instrument they're using while they try to sell the first one. Even so, he says, "If you find the instrument of your dreams in a shop, you have to liquidate your first instrument."

Many musicians wishing to sell an instrument by consigning it or trading it in toward a better instrument will seek out the help of a dealer. This may be the dealership where you bought the instrument, where you'd like to purchase your next instrument, or simply where you've had work done on it over the years. Even if your current instrument is a commercial one that you bought through a catalog, you may still have established a relationship with a dealership where you've had repairs done or bought bows or accessories.

While you may feel that you have developed a positive business affiliation with a shop over the years, you should not assume that a dealer will be all that interested in helping you unload the instrument. A dealer has to be comfortable representing your

instrument to his or her clients. Kass' view is fairly typical: "If it's an instrument that we have not sold before,
we go through an extensive inspection process. We
have to be confident in the provenance, authenticity,
condition, and general reliability of the instrument. If
any of these factors make us uncertain, we'd prefer not
to handle it."

If a dealer decides to take your instrument in trade or purchase it outright, the offer you get will generally be no more than 50 percent of retail.

If your current instrument is by a contemporary
maker, consigning the instrument with that maker
may be your best solution. Even though you won't gain instant liquidity, the maker
will probably be more motivated to sell it than a dealer. While it is certainly more
profitable for a maker to sell a new instrument than a consignment, Francis Kuttner,
a violin maker in San Francisco, says, "I like to have a hand in reselling my own
instruments so that I can see the condition and the setup before putting them back
on the market."

Some makers will use a dealer to help them sell their instruments. Bein & Fushi
in Chicago, for example, works with several contemporary makers and will accept
one of their instruments as a trade-in. Robert Bein is reluctant to take a contemporary instrument in trade by a maker he doesn't represent, however, unless that
maker has an established, national reputation. But as the supply of available antique
instruments dwindles, dealers are becoming more flexible. Paul Becker of Carl
Becker & Son in Chicago chooses contemporary instruments to sell very carefully,
but he is enthusiastic about their market potential. "You can buy one by an up-and-
coming maker now for the same price as a commercial instrument and, like a high-
risk stock, the upside can be tremendous."

The instant gratification of trading in is seductive, especially when you have
your heart set on your next instrument. But bear in mind that a dealer's level of
interest will depend on his current inventory and how quickly he thinks he can sell
it. Dealers stand to make far more profit selling an instrument they own, as opposed
to a consigned instrument, and they will select their investments carefully.
Inventory that sits around and doesn't turn over is a dealer's nightmare.

If a dealer does decide to take your instrument in trade or purchase it outright,
the offer you get will generally be no more than 50 percent of retail, and it may be
closer to one third that figure. To encourage customer loyalty and to save time and
money bringing instruments up to saleable condition, many of the large dealerships,
including Bein & Fushi and William Moennig & Son, Ltd., set a trade-in policy when
they sell an instrument. Bein says that if a client brings in an instrument he bought

at Bein & Fushi, "We guarantee a trade-in value of at least the purchase price." Moennig's dealers will use the most recent insurance appraisal they've written for an instrument purchased from them as the basis for the trade-in value toward your next purchase. Kass adds, "We usually require a small discount for a resale commission. However, if we know we have a ready buyer for the instrument and it needs little or no workshop time, we can (and often do) allow the entire appraised figure."

Consigning your old instrument is another means of selling it that is generally appropriate when you don't need the proceeds from that instrument to buy your next one. Dealer policies on consignment vary widely, and you should examine the agreement very carefully. Commission rates hover around 20 percent, with less expensive instruments sometimes commanding higher rates.

Some dealers will give you 80 percent of what the instrument sells for; others will give you 80 percent of what you agree upon as the asking price. McKean advises against consigning an instrument at an agreed-upon net return, since it could sell for more than you expect. Any return from a consignment, he says,

Dealer policies on consignment vary widely, so be sure to examine the sales agreement carefully before signing over your violin.

should be a percentage of the final sale, and you should be able to see the receipt from that sale.

Dealers will often insist that repair work be performed in order to bring a consigned instrument up to saleable condition. Policies on how this cost is absorbed also vary widely. While Wm. Moennig & Son's doesn't charge for any necessary repairwork, Carl Becker & Son's policy is more representative: they will itemize the cost of repairs if the work is estimated to exceed $300 and will deduct this cost from the payoff amount.

One drawback of consigning is that if your instrument has appreciated substantially, you have to pay capital-gains tax on the difference between your purchase price and selling price, minus selling costs such as the commission. When you trade in your old instrument and pay the balance in cash, however, the transaction is normally tax-exempt because it's considered a like-kind exchange.

Consigning can also be problematic because it takes an instrument out of your hands, and years can go by before it sells. Dealers are not motivated to accept 20 percent on the sale of an instrument that is consigned when they can make up to 200 percent profit on an instrument they own. Seemingly everyone has a story about a consigned instrument that has been allowed to languish. While, as Paul Becker admits, "less expensive instruments do have the potential to hang around for years," Becker's has a very player-friendly aspect to their consignment policy: if they own outright the instrument you'd like to buy, you may consign your old instrument but play on the new one in the meantime (eventual proceeds from the sale of the old instrument will go toward the cost of the new).

THE BARGAINING PROCESS

While dealers will go to great lengths to buy low and sell high, they also have an interest in working with you, the client. When you have an instrument to sell, there will be times when you can gain an advantage in the bargaining process. You will always have more leverage as a seller when you are also buying an instrument from the same dealer. Furthermore, the bigger the jump you're making in the market, the more bargaining room there is for both you and the dealer. If you approach a dealer with a $20,000 violin that you want to trade toward a $60,000 violin, you are justified in negotiating a trade-in value that is closer to $20,000 than if you were seeking to buy a $22,000 instrument. This is because the costs involved in selling the $20,000 violin are absorbed by the profit realized in selling a $60,000 instrument.

The rarefied atmosphere of a large, venerable violin shop, while thrilling, can also intimidate. Although the process of trading in a modern German violin toward a William Forster is not unlike trading in your Chevy for a new Audi, you may hesitate to drive the kind of hard bargain you would at a car dealership. While you can't research invoice figures for the Forster as you can for the Audi, you can still approach the transaction as an educated and knowledgeable consumer. Above all, leave your emotions at the door and be prepared to walk away from the deal if necessary. Like car dealerships, stringed-instrument dealers have a right to make a profit on what they sell. Don't forget, though, that whether you are trading, consigning, or selling your instrument outright, you're also entitled to a fair deal.

SOUND
YOUR BEST

SETTING YOUR VIOLIN UP RIGHT

by Julie Lyonn Lieberman

Imagine finding a way to hold your violin or viola that favors both your left- and right-hand activity, feels secure, doesn't make a mark on your neck, and provides the option of several head positions so that your body isn't locked into one position for hours and hours. It's available to you if you're willing to take the time to experiment with equipment until you create the optimum setup for your individual needs.

When we play, we are creating a frame between the left and right sides of our bodies, much the way two dancers must maintain an interrelated stance to move across the dance floor as a couple with grace and fluidity. We are all constructed differently, yet the types of equipment that help determine upper-body position and degree of muscular comfort are manufactured as if we're all cookies from only a few cutters.

Proper shoulder-rest placement can prevent unneccessary playing injuries.

The efficiency of your setup will determine how much freedom of motion you have when you play. An optimum setup won't cause a mark on your neck or collarbone. It also won't require a lift in the left shoulder or the tightening—and eventual injury—of the neck. In fact, with the appropriate chin and shoulder rests, you should be able to move your chin and shoulders freely, experiencing total freedom of motion in the left hand while feeling secure.

Many players search for one "correct" position and then faithfully maintain it for thousands of hours each year. I prefer to take a tai-chi approach, searching for a frame and support system in which the body has the flexibility to breathe by making constant, minute changes in position. Objects that are static become heavy. Once you've created a balanced and stabilized relationship with your instrument, you'll be free to shift the position of your head and neck constantly, as well as vary the levels of responsibility for the security of the instrument between left thumb, inner wall of the index finger, shoulder, collarbone, and chin. This, in turn, will reduce the perceived weight of the instrument.

Shoulder rests come in all shapes, sizes, and price ranges.

GETTING COMFORTABLE WITH YOUR INSTRUMENT

I've noticed that a number of teachers tend to recommend the products they them-selves use. This doesn't necessarily work. We're all different sizes and shapes, have varying levels of muscle tone, and differ tremendously in posture. I keep an arsenal of chin and shoulder rests in my music studio, along with a wood file and sandpaper, so that when I meet with students for the first time, we can try as many options as necessary to make them comfortable with their instruments. Depending upon body type, this may take a few minutes or a whole lesson, and it usually requires modification once they've had a chance to practice for a week using the new setup. I have yet to meet with someone for the first time and not have to make modifications. In fact, I can't tell you how many adult students have walked in the door using a child's chin rest (the circumference of the rest is the giveaway) or an old velvet shoulder rest that constantly slips and slides while they play.

The old argument that using any kind of support will reduce resonance isn't true. And besides, today's equipment has been designed to make contact only with the edges of the instrument. In fact, placing the violin directly on your shoulder— if you're lucky enough to have a stub for a neck—actually dampens resonance more than using a rest. But let's say, for argument's sake, that chin and shoulder rests dampen resonance by seven percent. That's a small price to pay, because what good is a fully resonating violin to a player who's in too much pain to play well?

The first step is to place the shoulder rest properly. The frame must favor ease of rotation of the left forearm, as well as the perpendicular placement of the bow to the bridge. How you angle the shoulder rest on the back of the instrument will swivel the fingerboard either away from or toward your fingering hand. As you swing your instrument to the left, you make it easier to rotate your forearm and bring your fingers perpendicular to the fingerboard. But if you go too far, you will have difficulty bowing between the fingerboard and bridge in a perpendicular motion while maintaining a relaxed right shoulder. On the other hand, if you swiv-el the instrument directly in front of you, it is harder to rotate the left forearm, which places an increased burden on the chin, jaw, and neck. This position causes the instrument to lean down, making you fight gravity to keep it up; at the same time, it forces your right arm back by your side. The rotator cuff, located where the arm attaches to the torso, wasn't designed to allow much freedom of motion when the elbow falls back by the side of the body, so chances are good that you'll devel-op tenderness or injury in the front of your right shoulder or rotator cuff, or compensate by breaking at the wrist while bowing at the frog to avoid excessive shoulder strain.

The shoulder rest can be placed straight across the back of the instrument, high on the left and low on the right, or low on the left and high on the right (or at one of numerous increments in between). Experiment with placement to avoid the problems mentioned above. It takes time to set up a shoulder rest correctly, so don't get frustrated. Many of the shoulder rests available today offer a number of options for height and placement, but the directions that come in the package are usually not worth reading. There are often two screws underneath. The longer screw should go over the shoulderer, enabling you to raise the rest to its maximum height and fill in the gap between your chin and shoulder. The shorter screw goes over the chest. Keeping the shoulder screw longer than the chest screw will allow you to tilt the face of the instrument toward the bow arm, so that you don't have to lift your arm too high to reach your lowest string.

Kadenza shoulder rests are popular because they're good at gripping the instrument.

Always remember that you are trying to create a frame that will enable the bow arm to activate the instrument without raising the right shoulder or placing the left arm too far forward. The final bargaining agreement between the two sides of your body will depend upon upper-arm length in relationship to lower-arm length, body size, neck length, shoulder width, and, in some cases, increasing demands on the healthy side of the body if an injury is healing on the other side.

FINDING THE IDEAL SETUP

Once you've analyzed your needs and feel ready to revamp your shoulder and chin rest situation, your first step, if you are addressing the setup on your own, will be to go to a large, well-stocked string shop and try out everything there (or order a number of options from a string catalog and return the rejects) until you find a comfortable solution. Even then, you may need to build height on the chin rest by placing foam pads on it, or by adding a layer or two of cork under the rest's feet, or by wrapping a piece of foam around the shoulder rest.

CUSTOMIZING YOUR SETUP

A mirror in which to watch your bow arm can help you determine placement of the instrument. Individuals with broad shoulders do better with a straighter shoulder rest, such as the Kun or the Bon Musica, and a broad chin rest. Individuals with narrower shoulders may require a centered chin rest and a curved shoulder rest, such as the Wolf Forte Secondo. In your player's tool kit, a wood file and some No. 10 sandpaper can come in handy to tailor the chin rest to your jaw size and shape, thereby alleviating any pain caused by a hump or lip on the rest.

If you are lucky enough to have a teacher who is skilled in these matters, you can expect to spend anywhere from 15 minutes to several lessons on your setup, depending upon the personal physical issues you are dealing with, such as injuries or an unusual body type. Unfortunately, many teachers are not equipped to deal with this fully—not because they don't care, but because they were trained in the "no pain, no gain" school and are simply lacking information in this area.

If, after trying to address these issues by yourself or with your teacher, you are still experiencing extreme discomfort while playing, then you will need to see a technique-rehabilitation specialist such as myself. Finding one can be tricky, though. You can ask a fellow string player or call a local music-medicine clinic. If you're lucky enough to live in or near Montreal or have frequent flier miles, you can go see violinist and luthier Peter Purich, who will spend several hours with you and design and hand-carve a chin rest for your exact dimensions and needs. He will be led by the specifics of your body, unlike companies dedicated to fabricating prototypes suiting the largest common denominator rather than the individual.

Whether you work on this on your own or with the guidance of a professional, after hours of sometimes frustrating experimentation you will finally arrive at the best solution for your body type. At last, you will feel extremely comfortable. Your playing won't create sores on your neck or collarbone. Your technique will feel freer, more fluid. You will be able to access several different head positions. And, most important, there will be a significant improvement in your tone. This is because you will have created the optimum positioning for both hands to work and for the instrument itself to sing out. Keep in mind that if you gain or lose weight, change instruments, or dress for winter versus summer, your setup may require slight modifications or even major changes.

THE PROPER
NECK ANGLE

by James N. McKean

A properly set neck is one of the most important components in an instrument's tone. The reason is simple: the neck has a profound effect on how much the instrument vibrates and how those vibrations are distributed. The body of your instrument is no more than a resonating chamber that amplifies the vibrations of the string when you bow it. The character and volume of the sound you get from your instrument are shaped by the way the body vibrates. The vibration of the string and the way the body responds to this vibration is determined for the most part by one thing: tension. The amount of tension on a string tuned to any particular pitch is determined by its length and mass. The longer the string, the more tension it will take to tune it up to pitch. Likewise, the more mass there is to the string, the more tension it will have. As mass is a measure of weight and volume, it is easy to see why gut strings are so much thicker than their steel counterparts. A string length that is too short will result in strings that feel flabby, requiring the use of thicker gauges that can give you a slower response and a feeling of general clumsiness. Strings that are too long will make the instrument sound wired, as though it has had too much caffeine, and make it more difficult to finger.

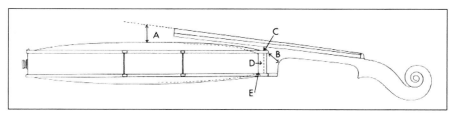

There are many factors to consider when setting the angle of the neck. (See text for explanation of violin angles labeled.)

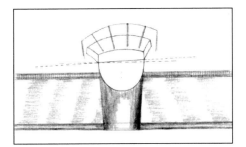

A properly placed neck is tilted in relation to the instrument's body in order to balance the sound of the strings.

The critical measurement in setting an instrument's neck is the distance from the side of the neck to the notches of the f-hole, which are intended to be a guide for the proper location of the bridge. (The foot of the bridge should be centered on the notch, exactly equidistant between the wings of the f-holes.) This measurement, known variously as the *stop*, the *mensure*, or the *diapason*, is important because the neck length is proportional to it—a proper neck-to-mensure length ratio is two to three for a violin. The distance between the curve of the neck heel and the edge of the top where it meets the neck (B in the diagram on page 77), is also keyed to the mensure. All of these measurements are so important because there are no frets on these instruments. The player's sense of where to shift to depends on a few markers, of which the neck heel is the most important. When you slide up to third or fourth position, you know where you are when your thumb reaches the neck heel. Of course, you can learn to adjust if these measurements are off, but if you do, you might find it difficult to play instruments of a more conventional design.

SOUND AND PLAYABILITY

The sound produced by the body of your violin is a result of what acousticians call resonance. When the strings vibrate, they cause a sympathetic vibration in both the wood of your instrument and the air inside the chamber. One important factor that affects the movement of the top is the amount of pressure exerted by the strings—and this depends on how steeply the neck is set.

The general rule is that the steeper the angle of the strings over the bridge, the more pressure will be exerted downward onto the top of the instrument. There is a range of angles that will work for any given instrument. There is no exact measurement or formula to go by; experience and intuition guide a maker to the setting that allows the instrument to sound its best. When you take an instrument to a violin maker, he or she will invariably put a ruler on the fingerboard and then measure straight down at the bridge. This is called the *renversement,* or pitch (A). The maker will also take a measurement (known as the *appui,* or overstand) at the mortise where the neck is set into the body, from the top of the edge to the edge of the fingerboard (C). With a quick glance at the saddle—the ebony bit at the other end, over which the tailgut rides—he or she can then get a sense of how much pressure is being exerted on the top. Too little, and the sound will be unfocused, with no sense of bite or depth. That's because there isn't enough tension directed downward and therefore not enough force to cause the bridge to rock as much as it might if the angle were steeper. On the other hand, if the neck is set too steeply, the result will be all edge and no richness. In this case there is so much pressure that the top can't move—it's locked up. While the height of the neck left standing over the edge at the mortise—the appui—is important for tonal reasons, it is equally so for a practical reason: if it is too low, you will bump into the edge as you shift into higher positions.

When holding your violin, take a close look down the fingerboard toward the body. You should see that the neck is tilted horizontally, so that the plane of the neck is not true to that of the body of the instrument (see diagram on page 78). The difference will be very slight, but if the neck has been properly set, it should be lower on the treble side. While the amount of tilt is less than a millimeter, the effect it has on both the sound and playability are noticeable. The latter is slightly eased as the fingerboard is rotated more toward the left hand, which curves somewhat unnaturally around the neck. The sound is affected in that the relative angles with which the strings cross the bridge is altered—lessened for the top strings and increased for the lower. This has the effect of evening out the sound. The lesser angle on the upper end will ease the tension and thus back the sound off a bit, while the increased angle of the lower strings translates into slightly more tension—resulting in what one of my customers calls "sizzle and pop."

ASSESSING NECK MOVEMENT

When considering neck movement in an old instrument, it is important to look at what sort of damage might exacerbate the problem. Cracks in the crown of the top (along the sides of the fingerboard or the tailpiece) should be examined carefully to ensure that they are well repaired and holding. It is also important that the top joint be secure. Although more difficult to ascertain, it is also helpful to know the thickness of the top in this area (a thin top will be more susceptible to the effects of weather).

Also important, and again difficult to verify, is the condition of the upper block (see D on page 77)—particularly how well it is joined to the top. The only way to check this is to knock down the strings and bridge, remove the endpin, and look inside with a good light. If you are considering buying an instrument and are at all concerned about its stability, it is well worth the effort. Simply put, the block has to be able to carry the load, which means it has to be wide enough to distribute the stress across a greater part of the ribs and plates. The older Italian makers were well aware of this; although Stradivari made the upper block quite shallow (not extending far into the cavity of the instrument), he made it very wide. Making the block shallow also meant that the graduations of the top and back could be brought farther out, helping to optimize vibration (E).

The fit of the block can be checked to some extent by the shape of the ribs adjacent to the neck, where they are glued to the upper block. If they are at all deformed, or if they don't appear to meet the neck and plates tightly, a close examination is in order to make sure this is not indicative of a serious problem. Since the ribs will shrink, it may appear that they are not securely joined at the block; this is where the expert eye is indispensable. A look inside will also reveal how securely the top is glued to the upper block. Considering how much this joint carries the stress exerted by the neck, it is of paramount importance that it be without a flaw.

How well the neck has been fit is also very difficult to establish, although again there are a few tell-tale clues for the experienced observer. The button—the little semicircle of the back that protrudes and covers the end of the neck heel—is of crucial importance to the stability of the neck. It acts as an anchor, holding the heel in place, and if it has been broken off, the neck cannot be considered secure. Older instruments with broken buttons or buttons that have been completely replaced are not uncommon; the correct way to repair a break, however, is quite involved. The button has to be doubled with new wood extending back into the block area of the back, so that the load on it is properly distributed. This involves removing the top, destroying the old upper block, making a counterpart for that area of the back, and then fitting a doubling of new wood. If properly done, the result can be virtually invisible. Many instruments have a semicircle of ebony finishing the edge of the button. Also known as a crown, it can serve a dual purpose—hiding the joint of a button doubling and enlarging a button that has been reduced through wear or bad repair over the years. Another way to assess the quality of the neck set is to run your finger around the purfling channel at the upper back; if it dips at the button, then the repairer slipped. The hot hide glue used to glue instruments together is tricky stuff; it is slippery and slick when first applied, but it begins to gel quickly. Because it is water based, it also causes the wood to swell, which changes the precise character of the joint.

FITTING AND SHAPING THE NECK

Fitting a neck is in itself a meticulous job, as it requires that the neck be set in a blind mortise (meaning that it is closed at one end, in this case by the button) and set at precisely the right length, angle, and tilt. It can take hours to get it right on an old instrument. Gluing the neck after fitting it, however, requires precision of a different kind; the maker has to brush the glue on, seat the neck, wrestle with the counterparts, clamp it, and clean off the excess glue before it mars the varnish. And the tolerance is less than half a millimeter. The glue has a hydraulic effect, on top of everything else; too much glue will force the neck back up out of the joint or prevent it from seating against the button. And if too much time is taken, the neck can jam before seating that last half millimeter. Instead of the end of the neck root being moved into its proper place against the back, the back gets pushed up to meet the end of the neck root, resulting in that little dip you sometimes feel.

Necks that are too small can have pieces added to them—glued on at the end to lengthen them, at the end of the heel to raise them, on the sides of the heel to widen them, and on the surface (under the fingerboard) to bring them up to proper thickness. At some point, however—either due to wear or breakage—they have to be replaced. A neck graft, while technically one of the most complicated jobs on an instrument, is frequently required. In fact, it is quite rare to find an instrument made prior to the mid–18th century that hasn't had the neck replaced. It was around the end of the 18th century that necks became longer and set at a steeper angle to increase the tension, and thus the projection and power, of the instrument.

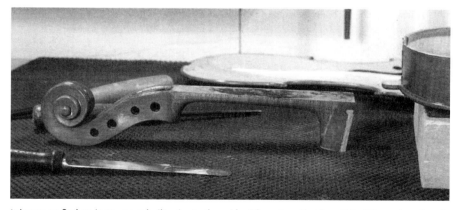

It is rare to find an instrument built prior to the mid–18th century that hasn't had its neck replaced.

There is no real mystery to the grafting procedure. Basically, the old neck is cut off and a new one of matching wood is fit. After the glue is dried, it is carved and set. One has to be careful not to crack the pegbox walls when gluing the new neck, but fitting it is much like setting the other end in the body after it's all done.

Shaping a neck is a true test of the carver's skill. The shape has to be as perfectly uniform as possible so that as the player shifts, he or she is not bothered by any irregularities. While carving the neck, the maker will use a lamp to throw a sharp shadow onto the neck; any wavering of the line, as he rotates the neck, indicates a bump or dip that has to be taken out. The widths and thicknesses are again measured in half millimeters, and the taper from the nut to the heel must be uniform. There are several different shapes that can be given to a neck; the difference is a matter of feel, rather than anything that can be measured. A neck that is too v-shaped will initially feel better, but over time the sharp edge of this type of neck will begin to bother most players. At the other extreme, a neck that is too oval will feel like a club. Measurements only tell a part of the story; a neck that is "too thick" can actually be thin—it's a matter of how the shaping is handled.

How much can be done to minimize the movement of the neck on your instrument—or to maximize the sound you're getting—is a matter for your repairer to determine. What you have to keep in mind is that the movement is, to a greater or lesser degree, inevitable. Movement, after all, is what makes the sound of the instrument; it's designed to be flexible—within reason, of course, which means a range of movement that doesn't interfere with your ability to play. If it's more than that, and it can't be reasonably taken care of, then it's time to move on. Remember, you are not a slave to your instrument; it is there to serve you. If it isn't working, and fixing it is too problematic or expensive, find another.

CHOOSING
STRINGS

by Richard Ward

Not long ago, I found an old catalog (circa 1960) from William Lewis & Son in Chicago when they were one of the largest violin shops in the world. I noticed the limited selection of strings available to musicians at the time. You could choose from a few steel-core strings, primarily designed for students, or gut-core. There were familiar names like Pirastro, Thomastik-Infeld, and Jargar along with others that have since disappeared. This was more than a decade before Thomastik-Infeld would introduce its revolutionary Dominant perlon-core strings.

Today there more kinds of traditional gut-core strings than there were 40 years ago, a dozen or so synthetic-core strings that are routinely stocked by the larger stringed-instrument specialists, and a multitude of steel-core strings. Most of these strings have been introduced in the last few years. The major string manufacturers are constantly introducing new products, which can be overwhelming and confusing for musicians. But a little knowledge will help you through the string-buying maze.

There are three different kinds of violin strings to consider, each with its own characteristic sound, feel, and

There are an overwhelming number of violin strings available in today's market.

response. I have included list prices, which are very broad—some varying as much as 50 percent. Here is an approximate guide for complete sets of violin strings: budget price, $12 to $40; mid-price, $20 to $50; and premium price, $40 and above (the overlap is due to a wide variance in dealer and list prices).

GUT-CORE STRINGS

Musical-instrument strings have been made of sheep or lamb intestine since the earliest days. Until the end of the 19th century, gut strings were the only strings available. On the violin, the E, A, and D strings were usually plain unwrapped gut. The G string has taken different forms to reduce mass, using forms of twisting, braiding, and wrapping. Today, musicians specializing in early-music performance are among the few using plain gut strings. Most who use gut-core strings use those that are wrapped with silver or aluminum.

Gut-core strings have their own unique sound, which is very full and complex with lots of overtones. Of all types, these strings have the slowest response. On many instruments there is a slight resistance, or "catch," on note or bowing changes, an effect that is more pronounced on some instruments than on others. Because they are lower in tension, gut strings tend to feel softer and more pliable under the finger. The major disadvantage is that they are rather unstable in response to temperature and humidity changes and thus tend to go out of tune frequently. When first installed, gut-core strings need about a week to stretch out before they have any kind of stability at all. Some musicians get tired of the constant tuning. The sound of these strings, however, can be beautiful, and although manufacturers of synthetic-core strings often claim their strings sound just like gut, they usually don't.

Pirastro's premiere gut-core string, Pirastro Oliv, has been on the market for almost 40 years. The sound is moderately brilliant with quick response for a gut-core string. You can dig in and get lots of sound from these excellent strings. The G string uses a gold alloy wrapping, and the E string is gold-plated steel with a beautiful, clear, and pure sound. Premium priced.

Pirastro Eudoxa strings have been on the market for a long time and were the standard string for many years. They have a dark, warm, and quite full sound. The response is rather slow, and they can sound dull on some (especially newer) instruments. Eudoxa strings work best on old German and Italian violins, especially those with a higher arching. Premium priced.

Plain gut strings can also be obtained from string maker Damien Dlugolecki (520 SE 40th St., Troutdale, OR 97060; www.teleport.com/~damian/strings.htm; [503] 669-7966). He makes all kinds of traditional gut strings, and has a good reputation. Premium priced.

Kaplan Golden Spiral and Golden Spiral Solo strings are made by D'Addario, one of America's largest string makers. I have found the sound to be similar to the Pirastro Gold. The solo version is a bit more brilliant and is available in different gauges. Both premium priced.

The Pirastro Gold is another old-timer. Less expensive than Olivs or Eudoxas, the Gold comes in only one gauge and has a sound somewhere between those of the other labels. The E string is one of the most popular on the market and works well with many other strings. Upper mid-priced.

Pirastro Chorda strings are made for early-music specialists with violins set up for Baroque performance. The E, A, and D are plain gut, and the G is wrapped with silver-plated copper wire. They are designed to be tuned to a 415 A. (The 415 A is one of many older—and lower—"standard" pitches. The lower pitch makes for a more mellow sound. Modern pitch in the U.S. is typically 440 hertz. In Europe the standard is sometimes higher—445 or 450—which gives the orchestras a more aggressive, brilliant tone.) Mid-priced.

SYNTHETIC-CORE STRINGS

In the early 1970s, Thomastik-Infeld revolutionized violin-string making by introducing Dominant perlon-core strings. The claim was that now you could have a string that sounded like a gut-core string but didn't have the disadvantages of pitch instability and slow response. These strings use a core of perlon (a type of nylon) wrapped with silver or aluminum. Within a day or two of installing the strings, they stretch out and stabilize. The core isn't affected by changes in temperature and humidity nearly as much as gut, so these strings stay in tune much better. They also have a quicker response. Since the introduction of Dominant strings, other manufacturers have introduced many new synthetic-core strings using not only perlon, but also high-tech composites such as Kevlar. Each string has its own particular sound quality.

Larsen has been making excellent cello strings for some time. When the company's violin strings came on the market, I was as impressed as I have ever been with new strings. They are powerful and brilliant but with great quality. The sound is noticeably bigger than that of the Dominant. The biggest problem so far is that the D and G strings tend to lose their quality rather quickly and suddenly. Premium priced.

Made in France by Saverez, producer of high-quality strings for tennis rackets, the Corelli Alliance uses a Kevlar core rather than perlon. The sound is warm and dark, although not as warm and dark as the Obligato, for example. These strings have a small but devoted following. Premium priced.

My initial trials of the Pirastro Evah Pirazzi have shown it to be an outstanding string. It's more brilliant than the Obligato (see below), silvery, powerful, and with a great deal of character. These strings need two or three days to stabilize, as they tend to stretch a great deal when new. Premium priced.

Thomastik-Infeld's Infeld Blue and Infeld Red strings are newer to the market. They are designed to complement one another; the tensions are the same, allowing you to mix and match. The Infeld Red set has a darker, warmer sound, and the Infeld Blue is more brilliant. In my preliminary tests, I found them to be excellent strings. The Blue set sounds a bit like Dominant strings but with more warmth. These strings also proved to have a shorter break-in period. Premium priced.

Thomastik-Infeld Dominants, the original synthetic-core strings, are still top sellers. The sound is brilliant and responsive, and these strings seem to work well with many different instruments. When they are first installed, they have a rather metallic and edgy sound that disappears with a few days of playing. The E strings don't seem to match the quality of the other strings, and many players substitute a Pirastro Gold E, which is a good match. Mid-priced.

Pirastro's first response to Dominant strings was the Aricore. This string has a dark, warm sound but can be dull and rather dead on some instruments. If you have a violin that is harsh and shrill, you might want to consider these strings, which are available only in medium gauge. In contrast to the Aricore, Pirastro's Synoxa is brilliant and focused. If your violin has a fuzzy tone, you might try this string (also available in medium gauge only). Mid-priced.

Until Pirastro introduced its Tonica strings, the company seemed to be having trouble competing with Thomastik-Infeld Dominants. Tonicas are excellent strings with a bright sound. The sound is not as bright as that of the Dominant, but it has more complexity, fullness, and depth. Some people may find the string to have a slightly slower response. Two E strings are available, one plain steel and one with aluminum wrapping.

I've found the wrapped E to be very useful on violins, but it has a tendency to squeak when going to the open E. Mid-priced.

When Super-Sensitive Sensicores were first introduced, they had a nice, brilliant tone—slightly less bright than Dominants. More recently, Super-Sensitive Strings introduced its professional-level perlon string, the Sensicore, in late 2000. The strings fare better in the lower register, building a deep, warm tone and good volume. But the A and E strings tend to be more shrill. Mid-priced.

D'Addario Pro Arte strings are usually priced a little lower than Dominants or Tonicas. The sound is fairly dark and smooth, making them a useful choice for bright, rough-sounding instruments. The D'Addario Zyex has a bright, focused quality and must be played for a few days before it reaches its optimum sound.

Although Dogal has been making strings in Venice, Italy, for more than 50 years, the company is not well known in this country in spite of its recent ad campaign. In fact, if you want to try Dogal strings, be prepared for a long search. When I first installed Dogal Synthetic Gut on my violin, I found them rather dull sounding, with a sluggish response. After two days, they seemed to perk up. I would characterize the sound as slightly dark, with slower-than-average response. I think Dogal needs to improve the D string (silver winding instead of aluminum would help) because of the flat, sluggish sound. The selling price is in the upper budget range.

When Pirastro introduced the Obligato, I found them to be one of the more interesting strings on the market. Of all the synthetic-core strings, the Obligato comes the closest to sounding like a gut-core string, namely the Eudoxa. Obligatos are, however, more responsive and slightly more brilliant. If you have a violin that would work well with Eudoxas, you might want to try the Obligatos. I would also suggest them for overly bright instruments. The standard set includes a silver-wrapped D and a gold-plated E. Budget priced.

Corelli Crystals have a tone that is warm and dark, with a fair amount of edge that keeps them from sounding too dull. When you take them out of the package, you will find them very stiff compared to other strings. They also feel thick under the finger, although they really are not thicker than any other string. Budget priced.

STEEL-CORE STRINGS

Steel strings began to appear in the late 19th century with the introduction of the steel E string (most E strings still employ steel in their creation). The A, D, and G strings use a core of fine strands of steel covered with a variety of metals, including chrome steel, silver, tungsten, titanium, and others. Many (but not all) steel-core strings have a tendency toward brightness. The sound is usually clear but simple, with few overtones. Steel-core strings have the fastest response of any string. Most are higher in tension and thinner than other types of strings. The least expensive of them tend to be edgy, tinny, and a bit rough. The best are of a much higher quality. With steel cores, there is very little expansion or contraction during temperature and humidity changes, and they tend to stay in tune better than synthetic-core strings. They are therefore a good choice for beginning students.

Thomastik-Infeld Spirocores have a very bright, hard-edged sound. They have a following among some nonclassical (country, bluegrass, mariachi, etc.) players. Thomastik-Infeld Ropecores, on the other hand, have a very dark sound with very little edge. For years Zeta, the maker of electric violins, recommended these strings for all its instruments. Mid-priced.

The D'Addario Helicore is a popular string with a smooth, warm tone. It has a soft, pliable feel under the fingers, unlike most other steel-core strings. It is probably the best choice for electric violins. Mid-priced.

If you play country, Cajun, or rock, Swedish Prim strings might be a good choice because of their power and ability to project. Their bright, edgy sound and low price make them popular. Mid-priced.

The Super-Sensitive Red label strings have a wide acceptance with schools and some beginning students because of their durability, very low price, and wide availability. Mid-priced.

Many decades ago, Jargar strings became popular with cellists, especially for the A and D strings, and with violinist for the A string. They have a warm sound and enjoy a good following, even with some classical musicians. Mid-priced.

The Pirastro Piranito is among the least expensive violin strings on the market, but has a surprisingly good sound for its low price. I find Piranitos useful for small student instruments. The Pirastro Chromcor is a step up from the Piranito but still budget priced. Chromcors have a bright, clean, and clear sound. They are also good with small student instruments. Pirastro's Flexocore strings have a warm, dark tone like the Helicore. Budget priced.

INSTALLING AND CARING FOR STRINGS

When trying a new type of string, reserve judgement for a few days. Most brands take time to settle in and reach their peak. After that, take them off and try something else. It may take some time experimenting to find the string best for you. Keep in mind that synthetic-core strings lose some of their quality when they are taken off an instrument and later reinstalled.

When you need to change an entire set of strings, do not remove all of the old strings at one time—you could loose the correct bridge placement. Also, lack of ten-

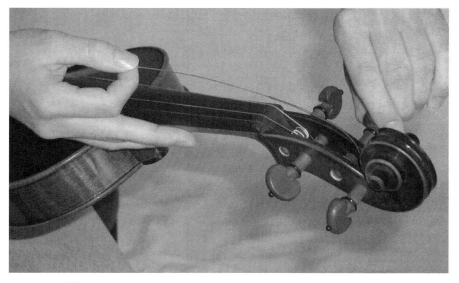

Removing a full set of strings at one time can collapse your soundpost—focus on one string at a time to avoid damaging your instrument.

sion can cause the soundpost to fall, something no violinist wants to be faced with. Remove only one string at a time, and keep all the others up to pitch. Tighten the string only up to pitch so as not to weaken the string. Thread the string through the hole in the peg, and wind it evenly from the center of the peg to just before the edge of the pegbox. Sometimes relatively new strings may break after installation; if this happens, be sure to take note of where the string broke. A violin can develop a rough spot at the peg, the nut, or the fine tuner. And if the winding of the string is too close to the wall of the pegbox, it may be under too much tension and stress, causing it to snap. Lubricating the grooves on the nut and bridge with a no. 2 pencil will reduce the chance of string breakage.

If you find that a peg keeps slipping, causing the string to go out of tune, it probably doesn't fit and needs to be replaced. A temporary fix would be to remove the peg and use standard blackboard chalk (or a mixture of peg dope and powdered rosin) on the peg where it touches the pegbox. But pegs that don't fit can eventually cause cracks in the peg box—an expensive repair. Changes in temperature and humidity can also cause the pegs to slip and pop.

Remember that once installed, strings slowly deteriorate. Usually within six months, they lose much of their tone quality and begin to sound dull and dead. This occurs even when the instrument isn't being played. Even unused strings in their package lose their quality. Over time the synthetic or gut core dries out and the metal wrapping can erode.

Often, trying different strings can go along way toward improving the sound of your instrument. But I must stress two things. First, every instrument responds differently to different strings, and the only way you can know for sure what might work for you is to experiment with different strings. Second, you can't turn a poor-sounding violin into a fine instrument just by changing strings. You can complement the good qualities or mask some faults, but the basic overall quality will come through no matter what string you use. Think of trying different strings as fine-tuning your instrument to get the best sound possible.

AMPLIFYING YOUR
ACOUSTIC VIOLIN

by Stacy Phillips

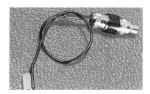 

Today, a number of manufacturers offer pickups for amplifying
violins. Shown are piezoelectric pickups from Ithaca and L.R.
Baggs (top) and a clip-on pickup from Fishman Transducers
shown mounted and unmounted.

Violins have long been omitted from the front lines of America's commercial music
(country music excepted). Research into amplification typically has been related to
solid-body electric guitars, which use magnetic pickups (a type of transducer that
converts sound vibrations traveling through a magnetic field into a small electric
current). The tone of early violin pickups left a lot to be desired.

The Barcus-Berry company pioneered improvements in violin pickups by introducing piezo-electric transducers, which transform pressure differences in the element (caused by vibration of strings, bridge, or body) into electric current. These are

now the most popular transducers for all acoustic stringed instruments. They can be quite sensitive to mysterious hums, ringing open strings, and any slight rustling or bumping of your violin. They amplify *everything*.

Historically, there have been actual and perceived limitations to amplifying using contact violins or, as they are more commonly called, temporary pickups (which touch the instrument, unlike a microphone). At one time, for example, the mere weight of the pickup element negatively affected the acoustic tone of the instrument, so no one wanted a permanently mounted device. This drawback has been largely eliminated with the advent of very lightweight transducers. Pickups never had the ability to deliver the variations of tone that subtle differences of bow speed and pressure can produce, and that still tends to be a problem. However, most gigs that require electric setups involve such a high stage volume that delicate effects are lost anyway. Often a cheap, solidly built instrument works wonderfully well with a good pickup and amplifier. But a pickup that works beautifully with one instrument and amplifier may not be the best choice with a different combination.

Most pickups also require peripheral equipment, such as a preamplifier and, less frequently, an equalizer, in addition to an amp that may be providing all your sound or, paired with a public address (PA) system, functioning only as a monitor or fill-in. An equalizer is used to control and shape the frequency spectrum of the instrument. Preamplifiers are necessary because most amplifiers are made for guitars with magnetic pickups, which require different impedance—the alternating-current (AC) equivalent of direct-current (DC) resistance—than piezo crystals. Preamps are necessary with piezos because their low and very high impedance does not work well with typical amplifiers. Preamps allow the crystals to deliver sufficient signals, thus matching impedance with the amplifier and avoiding loss of low frequencies. (That low-frequency loss was what produced the typical problem for the electric violinist of 20 years ago—tinny sound.) Both the preamp and the equalizer can help create equal signals from all strings. But if you are fortunate, with stage volume sufficiently controlled, a decent sound system, and a monitor in which to hear your-

AVOIDING FEEDBACK

If you're going to be playing at very high volumes, consider avoiding feedback by buying a solid-body electric violin instead of simply placing a pickup on your acoustic fiddle. Alternatively, you can alleviate feedback problems somewhat by stuffing your f-holes with foam rubber. This, of course, ruins the acoustic tone, but the effect is negligible on what comes from your amp.

self, you may be able to plug directly into the PA, eliminate the other gear, and still be audible.

PICKUPS

Currently, the best method of mounting a pickup is to fit a plug and jack to the side edge of the violin with the same type of clamp connection a chin rest uses. It does not interfere with the acoustic sound. The mini-size plug, which used to be standard, is more expensive to replace and more fragile. There is usually additional cost with the ¼-inch jack, and some companies do not send it assembled, so some intelligent soldering may be necessary, but an extra $20 is well spent on this so-called Carpenter jack (named for Fred Carpenter, a great fiddler who perfected it).

Today, there are a wide variety of pickups to choose from, from temporary contact pickups (attached to the instrument with adhesive) to permanently installed bridge pickups. The designs vary greatly. Some utilize a magnetic transducer, which requires metal or metal-coated strings and cuts down on bow sounds (as compared to a piezo transducer). Some sense string vibration with piezo-electric elements, others with lightweight microphones that are attached with a chin-rest–type rig, and others with combinations of different sources and blenders that allow you to adjust the mix (so that your signal is, say, 40 percent pickup and 60 percent microphone). In my experience, permanent, in-bridge violin pickups have the best overall responsiveness, and any kind of piezo pickup can generally be counted on for a strong bow-attack sound.

All pickups sound best when played through a PA system, which has a fuller range of frequency of response than traditional guitar amplifiers. Which pickup is best for you depends on what percentage of your work requires electronic reinforcement, how loud the rest of your group is, the kind of tone you are looking for, and what other equipment you use—instrument, amp, preamp, volume pedal, etc. Though electromagnetic pickups do not feed back as easily, piezos give truer tone.

If you choose a temporary pickup, make sure it's attached securely. Those that use some sort of adhesive must be attached with just enough goop for a firm fit but not so much as to dull the signal. The signals they produce are not as "hot" as the signal a built-in model provides, but for low-volume gigs, they can deliver very reasonable acoustic timbre. (The hotter the signal, the more signal is coming out of the pickup, so the volume knob on the amp need not be turned up as much as with a pickup with a weaker signal.)

AMPLIFIERS

Once you have settled on the specific electric pickup and style of violin (acoustic or solid-body), the job is only half done. The method of amplifying and otherwise altering the acoustic information produced by the pickup (and carried by electric current) is critical to the quality of sound. If stage volume is relatively reasonable (below ear-blowing pop-music level), you might be able to plug directly into a mixing board that controls the PA system. Otherwise, an amplifier is needed to deliver your playing to the audience.

For smaller rooms, you can use an amp as the sole source of sound. You can also connect your amp to the PA, and split the signal between the amp and PA so you can use the PA to reach the audience and your amp solely as a monitor. You can connect to the PA through a direct box, by miking the speaker, or by using a line out of the amplifier. Direct boxes are a lot like preamps, in that they match impedance between pickup and PA systems. A powered direct box can also match impedance between pickup and the instrument amplifier. The box also splits the signal between the PA system and the amp—each has its advantages, and your group's particular setup will dictate the choice. These choices may make more difference to the soundman than to the performer—and again are ruled by personal preference.

The most important part of an instrument amplifier is the speaker or speakers (there is often more than one in a "cabinet" or "box"). Generally, the better they are, the heavier. Few players want to carry around 40 pounds' worth of magnets, however, so each player must find his own compromise. Most commercial amps are combos that contain an amplifier and speakers in an acoustically designed box or cabinet. An alternative is to separate these two components and thus divide the weight into two lesser hauls. The tone (and tone control) can be superior this way, but the expense is greater. Tube amps give the warmest sound, but they are the heaviest and start to

The Zeta E-Series Amplifier was designed specifically for the sound of electric bowed instruments.

distort when the volume is pushed. (Some folks, especially electric guitarists, like a slightly fuzzy tone.) If you favor a tube amp, you need to get one with more power than you need. The added headroom will avoid distortion.

When you're ready to test some amps, try to get to a music store when it first opens. You can count on few customers and thus a chance to try a few models with the volume cranked up. Experiment with the controls to get an idea of what they do to the sound. Different setups produce varying amounts of bow noise, and most tend to accentuate the boominess and sustain of open strings.

Though there are amps advertised especially for acoustic instruments, only the most high-priced, high-end models really work. And in most cases, they are tailored for acoustic guitars. Buyers beware: there is a lot of sales hype out there.

EFFECTS

A few effects are standard fare. Reverb (most often delivered in digital) and delay (either analog or digital) are used to approximate the persistence of sound in acoustic settings. Dead rooms require more. Experiment. Commercial units usually have dozens of different settings. Delays repeat the original signal at prescribed intervals, from milliseconds to long enough to enable you to play a round or fugue with yourself. You can vary the percentage of presence of this processed signal as well as how many echoes you wish to hear, and you can change your settings from tune to tune.

Additional effects boxes are somewhat more esoteric. As a wah-wah pedal is depressed, the amount of high frequencies continually changes, resulting in a crying sound. An octave divider enables you to play one or two octaves lower and to mix the resulting pitches.

STAGE SETUP

You have to arrange your kit so that you can hear yourself. This can be a problem when performing with a drummer and electric bass and guitars. Usually as soon as you get enough monitor volume, the dreaded whine of feedback occurs. If you stand too close to a sound source (e.g., your amp or a PA speaker), various types of sonic loops can occur through your instrument. In addition, the natural resonance frequencies of the air chamber of acoustic instruments can begin howling when stimulated by enough vibration from your amp. Place your body between the amp and violin.

Most players like to have their speakers or monitors raised up and pointing toward their ears. If the amp is on the floor and the speakers point at your legs, you wind up playing louder than necessary. Bandmates react by cranking up their volume, and things get out of control. Put your amp on a chair and use a book or a small box to tilt it upwards.

Don't skimp on the wires that connect your equipment. Spending a few extra dollars saves you the heartbreak of hums and buzzes from fluorescent lights and poor electrical wiring. Perpendicular plugs can help you keep things streamlined. There also is a wireless route. Wireless systems actually do have a wire from the pickup to a transceiver (that can be clipped to your belt or pocket), which sends signals via the FM radio band to a box that is wired to your amplifier or sound system.

Wires, bandmates, and small stages all increase the danger of damaging your violin. To avoid having the instrument knocked out of your hands when someone steps on a wire, loop the cable over your shoulder or around your shoulder rest and then around your belt, with some slack to absorb jolts. Most accidents happen during breaks, so find a safe place for your instrument between sets.

Eric Aceto, a musician and builder of solid-body bowed instruments, says, "A good sound is one that the instrumentalist *believes* in. It's up to players to find their own sound and convince the audience. If you are willing to do the homework and spend the time, you can tailor the sound to the needs of your bowed instrument." Keith Barry, an outstanding jazz violist, who performs in many genres, elegantly sums up the reasons for amplification: "I believe the reason to amplify an acoustic instrument is to facilitate articulation at required volume levels, not simply to be loud."

PRESERVE AND PROTECT YOUR INVESTMENT

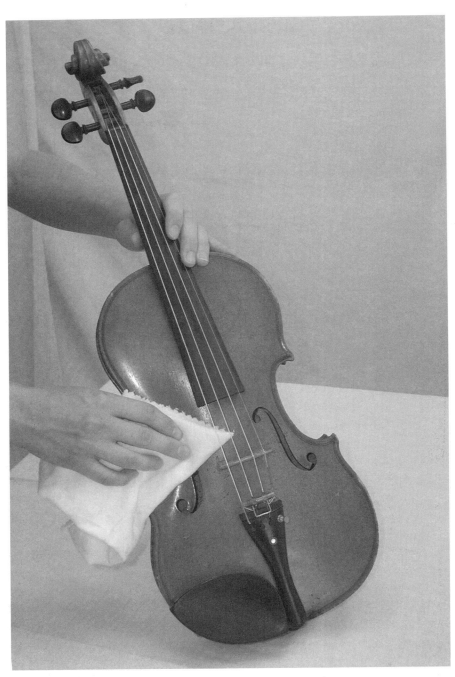

Preventing rosin build-up is the first step in keeping your instrument clean.

CLEANING AND CARING FOR YOUR VIOLIN'S FINISH

by James N. McKean

One of the most common questions players ask makers and repairers is how they can best take care of the varnish on their instrument. While there are things you can do, cleaning and polishing is something to be left to a professional. The better a violin varnish is, the more fragile—it has to be, to allow the wood to vibrate freely. The problem is that any cleaner effective enough to remove the buildup of dirt and rosin can sometimes also dissolve the varnish underneath. It's extremely difficult to know where one ends and the other begins, and while it can be retouched, once the varnish is gone, it's gone. It's worth bearing in mind that the freshness of the varnish contributes significantly to the value of your instrument, be it old or new. Commercial cleaners and polishes are best avoided—they are usually a combination of wax and linseed oil, which will build up and harden, trapping dirt and resulting in a second varnish that is very difficult to remove.

KEEPING YOUR VIOLIN CLEAN

There's still a lot you can do to keep your instrument clean. The best approach is to stop the dirt and rosin from building up in the first place. This means using a very soft cloth to wipe it off when you are done playing. Not just the rosin from the fingerboard and under the bridge, but also the sweat and dirt, which is usually on the top of the instrument. Try to get the perspiration before it dries—the salt is amazingly corrosive and will eat right through the finish. And even though you start with clean hands, dirt will build up very fast, particularly on the edges of the back and top at the shoulder. Get as much of the rosin as you can, but don't be a fanatic about it; rosin is an abrasive. An old cotton undershirt or handkerchief does very well for this. The soft buffing of the cloth will also give your instrument a subtle sheen that you would never get with polishes, which leave your fiddle looking like a new car in a showroom or a Christmas-tree ornament. The great varnishes aren't glossy to begin with, and it is a shame to see them end up that way.

You can clean the fingerboard yourself, but be very, very careful if you do. The only effective cleaner is alcohol, which is a solvent for most varnishes. It's difficult to control, because it can run all over the place. The trick is to use it sparingly. A folded pad of paper towel with just a dab from the can is enough; even better are the sterile, pre-moistened pads from the pharmacy. Before you even start, though, make sure the instrument is protected against any drips or runs. This is very easy to do. Never clean the fingerboard when you are holding the instrument up by the neck. Lay it flat on a table, with a towel under it and another rolled up under the button on the back so that it's stable and doesn't roll around. If you have to, put another support under the back of the scroll. The most important thing, though, is to put some thick cardboard over the top and under the fingerboard, reaching from the butt of the neck inlay to the front of the bridge. That way, if anything drips, it won't get on the varnish. You can clean the strings that way, too. To get at the fingerboard under the strings, gently pull them aside one by one. Don't loosen them, though—that might cause the bridge to shift or pull forward when you tighten them back up.

NICKS AND SCRATCHES

No matter how carefully you clean your instrument, however, the varnish and underlying wood will still be vulnerable to other kinds of damage. In the course of being played, your instrument will inevitably pick up nicks and scratches, and certain areas of the varnish will wear down. Some varnishes wear much faster than others or show the effects of bumps and scrapes more. And again, perspiration contains a lot of salt, which can corrode the varnish, the wood itself, and even the strings.

The areas that tend to wear fastest are the upper right rib and the edges where you shift into higher positions and where it is natural to hold a violin when you aren't playing it. Another area that wears quickly is the lower left rib and back, where the instrument is held against your neck while you play. New varnish is frequently applied to all these places and to any other where the wood has been laid bare, even on the most valuable instruments. The proper (easily removable) varnish must be used, and the wood underneath must first be thoroughly cleaned of dirt and oil and then smoothed, or the new varnish will not adhere. It is, of course, better to attend to this before you get to the bare wood, as it is a lot easier to replace lost varnish than wood.

This Giovanni Dollenz violin shows how the oil in your hands can wreak havoc on an instrument's varnish. Note the wear around the neck heel.

If you do wear through the new varnish on the shoulder and edges quickly, you might consider having a very thin piece of plastic tape applied to the varnish to protect it. It is frequently used on the ribs, particularly on valuable instruments where it is important to preserve as much of the original wood and varnish as possible. It can even be placed over the edges that are most susceptible to wear. The plastic is hardly noticeable if applied correctly, and it has no effect on the sound. It is easily removed without any damage to the varnish or wood underneath.

As for nicks and scratches, they happen all the time, and you can console yourself with the thought that they always look a lot worse than they are. They can be filled and retouched so that they are, at worst, hardly visible; they may not even be noticeable at all. The important thing is to keep the scratched area clean. Do not put tape over the nicks and scratches to protect them, because the adhesive on the tape will get into the bare wood and also might be hard to free from the varnish.

These scrapes and scratches are most noticeable on new instruments, where they really stand out. They can be retouched, but it is best just to relax and let them accumulate; after all, it is the wear that contributes to the beauty and allure of older violins. Like lines in a face, scratches add character, and they are an inevitable part of aging. Current taste calls for an evened-out look that requires extensive overvarnishing and polishing, which destroys the texture and patina of great old varnish. The result is a glassy, monochromatic finish that has effectively robbed the instrument of its warmth and individuality. If you are lucky enough to have a fine old instrument, do not let an overzealous repairer sell you on the idea of no imperfections and a high shine; once there, you can never go back, and you will have sacrificed one of the most valuable aspects of your instrument.

A NOTE ON THE NECK

The neck of an instrument both is and isn't varnished. The neck gets so much more wear than the rest of your instrument that it has to be finished differently. Even though your contact with the shoulder and edges is at best intermittent, they still suffer wear; the neck, by contrast, gets use every time you pick the instrument up. Any varnish will disappear quickly, and if it's the same as the varnish on the instrument, it will leave the neck feeling rough and uneven under your hand as it goes. It can be a most annoying and unpleasant sensation. Musicians are sensitive to the slightest irregularity in the feeling of the neck, and playing on a semiworn, heavily varnished one would be like driving too fast down a gravel road.

The neck does have a finish applied to it, though. The bare wood is sanded smooth and then wetted to raise the grain, which is done to

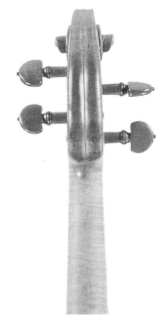

Violin necks, such as the one seen on this Guiseppe Rocca instrument, are finished with a combination of stain and linseed oil.

the rule of three. This means that after the third wetting and sanding, the water no longer swells the wood; the swelling raises the fibers and makes the surface feel rough. Once the neck is smoothed with 600-grit sandpaper (which results in a surface like polished marble), a stain is applied to darken the wood—usually chicory, boiled in water. Earth colors—burnt sienna, umber, and ochre, combined to match the undercoat of the instrument—are then mixed into linseed oil and rubbed into the neck with a rag. Enough is applied to fill the pores of the maple, and then the wood is polished the same way you polish your shoes. The excess comes off, and the wood is left looking dark and burnished and feeling perfectly smooth.

A retouching varnish—basically shellac—is used to build up varnish on the neck root (the part where the neck is joined to the body) and the heel (where it joins the scroll). However, this varnish fades out right at the angle of the neck proper. The rest of the neck is quickly brushed with one or two extremely thin coats, which are then polished vigorously. The heat anneals the thin varnish, working it into the pores of the wood, and leaves the neck protected with an undetectable layer of varnish for you to wear through as you play.

This finish will last for a considerable time for most players. You won't need to have it freshened up any more often than, say, you have the instrument cleaned. If, however, you are one of those unfortunate souls with particularly abrasive perspiration, you might cut through to the raw wood again in days. Your local repair expert might then have to resort to a more durable varnish for that last thin layer.

HUMIDITY AND YOUR VIOLIN

by David Burgess

One of the most important things you can do to protect your violin is to maintain proper moisture levels. Aside from accidental impact, more acoustic stringed instruments are brought in for repair because of improper moisture content than for any other reason.

Wood is a hygroscopic material, meaning that it absorbs moisture from the air. Like most water-absorbing materials, wood swells when it absorbs moisture and shrinks when it loses moisture. The moisture content of your instrument will generally depend on the moisture content of the surrounding air. If the humidity is high, your instrument will absorb water. If it is low, the instrument will lose water. As your instrument gains and loses moisture, its individual parts get larger and smaller. The variation is much greater than you might imagine.

Wood is much more flexible when it has a high water content. Instrument makers and repairers apply water, heat, or both to bend wood. (The ribs on your violin were formed this way.) A combination of high moisture and pressure from the strings will cause any violin to distort over time. No doubt you've seen some of these distortions, such as instruments that have bulged under the tailpiece and fingerboard and are sunken at the bridge. At 90 percent humidity, your instrument's resistance to bending is reduced by about 25 percent. No wonder it sounds different when you take it to a different climate. But worse, the resistance to bending under a sustained load (string tension) drops even more than 25 percent, which can bring down the neck projection and require the neck to be reset.

Relative humidity is a measure of how much water vapor is in the air, compared to how much the air can hold before becoming saturated. At 50 percent humidity, the air is holding half as much moisture as possible before condensing into droplets (dew or rain). Relative humidity varies with temperature. Warm air (which has high molecular activity) can hold more moisture than cold air. When warm air with a high mois-

104

An in-case hygrometer and humidifier can prevent the wood of your violin from cracking. A hygrometer will read the level of humidity around your instrument, and a humidifier can provide moisture when your violin needs it.

ture content cools, it can no longer hold all the moisture, and some of the moisture condenses. This is what happens when dew forms at night. (If you see dew on the grass in the morning, you can be sure that the humidity level outside came close to 100 percent.)

By the same token, if you take cold air and heat it, the capacity to hold moisture increases. If you take outside air at zero degrees Fahrenheit and 100 percent humidity, and you heat it to 70 degrees with the heater in your car or house without adding moisture, you will wind up with a relative humidity of about eight percent. This explains why the air inside your house is usually dry in winter.

High temperatures, by the way, are another serious danger to your instrument, and not only because of the drying tendency due to the surrounding hot air. Wood will lose 20 to 50 percent of its strength at 150 degrees as compared to room temperature. In addition, all varnishes become softer when exposed to heat. Many will become soft enough at 90 or 100 degrees to cause fabric impressions from the case to be left in the varnish. Even if the air temperature is within safe limits, an instrument can become very hot in direct sunlight simply from radiant energy.

CONTROLLING HUMIDITY

To control humidity levels, you must first find out the moisture content of the air. There are devices designed to help you do this. One is the dial-type hygrometer, which is available in hardware stores. It has been my experience that these are not very accurate. I once saw a dozen of them (all the same brand) on a shelf, and the readings varied by as much as 30 percent. I recommend Radio Shack's electronic, digital hygrometer/thermometers, which sell for about $30, will fit in most cases, and are quite accurate.

Test the humidity in your home or wherever you store or play your instrument. The target range for humidity is 40 to 60 percent. Going back to your heated house in winter, you might find the humidity to be about 20 percent. But it's winter and it's raining outside. Shouldn't the reading be close to 100 percent? Well, it would be, outside, but when you take that 35-degree air and heat it to 70 degrees, the heat sucks moisture out of the air and out of your instrument. That's why you probably need humidification if you live in a cold-winter area. If you live in a house, see about installing a central humidifier (if the hygrometer says that you need one). Not only will your violin appreciate this, but your piano, plants, and sinuses will as well. If you live in an apartment that ducts common air to many units, try putting a console-type humidifier in one room and keeping your instrument there with the door closed. (Your console humidifier is not capable of humidifying the entire building.)

AVOID THE SUN

Try not to expose your instrument, or the case containing your instrument, to direct sunlight, and never leave an instrument in a car or trunk. Aside from the risk you run of having your instrument stolen, temperatures inside a vehicle or the trunk of a car can easily reach 150 degrees on a sunny day.

A word of warning: in climates with very cold winters, it may not be possible to keep the humidity as high as 40 percent (the low end of your target range) in older buildings. If a structure is not well insulated with a good moisture barrier and insulated windows, the moisture you add from your humidifier could condense on cold surfaces, sometimes inside walls, and cause damage.

What if the humidity inside your home is too high? If the inside air is more humid than the outside air, as is often the case because of cooking and bathing, try ventilating the building. Air conditioners also act as dehumidifiers. You can also purchase a dehumidifier and keep it in a closed room with your instrument. Yes, they cost a

few hundred dollars, but if you need a humidifier or
dehumidifier and don't buy one, be prepared to spend
the money you save, and much more, on future repairs
to your instrument.

Test the humidity in your home or wherever you store or play your instrument.

If you travel a lot, there's not much you can do.
There are "humidity controlled" cases on the market
that feature internal instrument humidification
devices, but I have tested several that weren't very effective. I have also seen
evidence of water dripping from the type that are inserted in the f-holes, so be very
careful. During the time the violin is being played, there is so much air moving in
and out of it that they may make no appreciable difference. Make sure that any
claims are more than marketing or advertising hype. Perhaps you could test before
making a purchase. In order to be truly effective, I would expect that a case or
instrument humidity-control system would have to be capable of changing the
humidity in the case at least 20 percent from the level outside the case.

The bottom line is that rehearsal halls, performance halls, and other places where
valuable instruments are played or stored should be climate-controlled. Insist on it.
If enough people raise a fuss, maybe someone will listen.

CARING FOR YOUR BRIDGE, PEGS, AND FINGERBOARD

by James N. McKean

It doesn't take a lot to keep your violin functioning at its highest level. While most of what you can do is preventive, there are some parts that you can take an active role in caring for. The bridge is the heart of the instrument, the pegs the only movable parts, and the fingerboard the place you come in contact with the most. Understanding how they work and how to take proper care of them will go a long way to keeping you out of the repair shop.

THE BRIDGE

The cutting, fitting, and proper placement of your violin's bridge are critical to the sound and health of the instrument. The bridge blank is cut from specially selected, air-dried maple. Once a blank has been picked out, the feet are cut with a knife to fit the top perfectly, and then the crown is cut to give the strings the proper clearance off the fingerboard. This curvature is very important, as is the exact spacing of the notches for the strings; they will both affect the ease with which you can cross the strings or play one

A well-cut bridge can last for years before needing to be replaced.

without hitting another. The last step, planing it to its proper thickness and enlarging the cutouts with a knife, is the best way a repairman or maker has to fine-tune the timbre and response of your violin.

A well-cut bridge can last for years and years before needing to be replaced. You can enhance the life expectancy of your bridge by keeping it from warping. Warping is caused by the constant pressure of the strings, which gradually pulls the top of the bridge forward and stretches the wood out of shape. This is pretty easy to avoid—it's almost always due to changing all the strings in one sitting. If all four strings are new, the bridge will get pulled forward as you tune and then retune while the strings are stretching out. Replace them one by one, and let each stretch fully before moving to the next. Before you put the new string on, use a sharp pencil on the notch; the graphite will act as a lubricant. If the bridge does pull forward, then go to the shop and ask them to show you how to pull it back so that it's straight. It's not that hard, but it's tricky, and if you try pulling the bridge back without proper instruction, it might break or fall down. Then, with the high tension of the strings, the tailpiece will slam into the top, gouging and perhaps cracking it. Your repairer can show you how to pull it back and would much prefer to take the time to do so than make a new bridge or repair your top.

Another part to keep an eye on is the parchment glued to the bridge over the grooves for the upper strings. Since they're so thin, these strings can quickly saw through the unprotected maple of the bridge. Check the parchment as you change strings—if it appears to be worn through, get it replaced at once.

You can change the bridge yourself, as long as you exercise caution. Again, have your repairer show you how to do this. You'll need a bridge jack (most shops and mail-order concerns stock them). It's easy, once you've been shown how—but whenever you do it, make sure you always put some protection between the tailpiece and the top. Under no circumstances try to change bridges without a jack. The soundpost is only wedged in between the top and the back, and without the pressure of the strings, it might fall down. (If it does, you need a new soundpost, but that won't help you when the old one is rattling around inside). You can also damage the top if the bridge doesn't go exactly where it's meant to—the feet are cut to fit the top precisely, and the edges are sharp. Ideally, the bridge stands so that the notches of the holes, if connected, would run through the feet, which are exactly in the middle between the arms of the two soundholes. However, bridges are often not exactly in that spot, for sound or ease of playing. It's important for you to know where the bridge should be on your instrument, so you can tell if it's moved. This is something your repairer can show you; often there are tiny marks that locate the bridge on the top.

THE PEGS

The pegs should turn easily and hold without needing to be pressed into the pegbox. If they're well-fitted, you should be able to tune with the violin under your chin while you're bowing to check. The pegs are cut with a taper that exactly matches the holes in the pegbox and then lubricated with peg dope, a commercially available product that, paradoxically, helps the pegs to hold and to turn freely. If the pegs squeak, or if on the other hand they are slipping, try a little peg dope. Just a touch of peg dope will do; it builds up in the peghole, eventually hardening like glass, at which point the pegs won't hold at all.

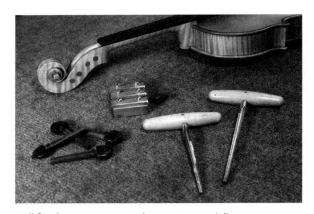

Well-fitted pegs can prevent damage to your violin.

Being made of wood, pegs and pegboxes are both susceptible to the vagaries of weather—in the summer they swell and the pegs will stick. In the winter they shrink, and you might open the case and find they have all let go overnight. Don't worry; retune the instrument, being very careful that the bridge is where it should be (this is one reason you should have your repairer show you where the bridge belongs on your instrument). First, though, check and make sure that the soundpost didn't fall when the strings went down.

A crack in the pegbox is a serious problem, one that is difficult and costly to repair. It's not that hard to avoid, though. One of the easiest ways, surprisingly enough, is as simple as winding the strings correctly. Do not wrap the string so it forces itself up against the pegbox wall. This might be necessary on a cheap, fractional student instrument, but never on anything approaching a decent violin. The peg is tapered, so it acts like a wedge; winding the string against the pegbox will force the peg deeper into the peghole, eventually cracking it.

The other cause of cracks (aside from banging the head) is forcing the peg to hold when it wants to slip. Pegs will compress into a mushroom shape over time, which makes them want to pop free. Pushing them in might open a crack in the pegbox from the pressure. If they aren't holding, or if they stick, it's time for professional help. Eventually, new pegs might be needed. If the holes get too large, or if they are so irregular they can't be trued with a reamer, then they have to be bushed, filled with wood, the varnish retouched, and new holes bored. New wood, either from bushing or on a new instrument, will most likely need a few applications of peg dope at first, as the wood is so absorbent. A little bit goes a long way.

THE FINGERBOARD

The fingerboard also requires regular attention. Even though it's ebony, which is a very hard and dense wood, it will still wear down with use. Dressing the fingerboard removes the grooves worn by the strings and hollows where your fingers rest. The board is planed, scraped, and then polished to a mirror smoothness. It's intentionally made slightly concave from end to end. Called the scoop, it provides additional clearance for the strings and helps prevent buzzing. The length of time between planings can be anywhere from one year to several, depending on the density of the wood, the amount you play, and how corrosive your perspiration is. Good ebony is becoming very difficult to find, so it is a good idea to go as

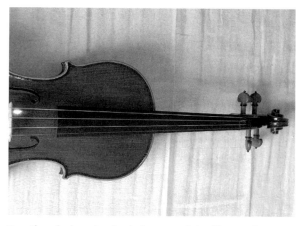

Even though ebony is a hard, dense wood, it still wears down with use.

long as you can between planings. At some point the fingerboard will be too thin to plane anymore and will have to be replaced, but if the instrument you have purchased has a healthy fingerboard, this should not be necessary for many years.

Preventative care and maintenance will keep your instrument playing its best and out of the repair shop for years to come. A little bit of care and attention on your part will pay off in large dividends.

PROTECTING
YOUR INSTRUMENT
FROM THEFT

by Jessamyn Reeves-Brown

Nobody really wants to think about the possibility of instrument theft. Oh, sure, you worry a little and hope it won't happen to you, but really, is it worth chaining your fiddle to your wrist? Actually, there are a lot of fairly simple things you can do to prevent theft and, in case the worst does happen, improve your odds of getting your instrument back. Use the following checklist to see if you're doing everything you can to safeguard your pride and joy.

1. Keep your violin in sight at all times. That means don't leave it in your car, don't check it as airline baggage if you can possibly help it, and don't think it's safe in the greenroom or backstage. Remember, it only takes a moment for a thief to snatch your case. If you absolutely *have* to leave it in the car, at least hide it from view, preferably locking it in the trunk (remembering to notice the temperature—the heat in a closed car or trunk can damage your instrument severely). And if you

Making sure your name and contact information are attached to your case—and even inside your instrument—may dissuade or help to catch a thief.

must check your instrument as baggage, gate-check it; it will be handed back to you when you disembark instead of left sitting in the baggage-claim area.

2. Pay attention. It's not enough to stay within a few feet of your violin if it could be taken without your noticing. Especially in crowded public places, be sure to keep a grip on the handle or to trap the case between your feet. And how many times have we heard about the instrument that was accidentally left on a bus, in a taxi, or—worst of all—on top of a car before driving away? Anyone who carries a purse knows that mere habit builds up a mental alarm system that goes off whenever the purse isn't there; if you consistently keep a close check on your instrument, the same thing will happen.

3. Label your instrument. What if you do leave your violin somewhere and an honest, well-meaning person finds it—will they be able to find you? It may seem obvious, but you need to make sure that your name and contact information are clearly marked on the outside of your case, and preferably also inside your case and even inside your instrument. This last is helpful if the violin goes astray, but also if it's stolen: a thief may not know to look into the f-holes, but a dealer or appraiser will. Make the name and phone number small, so only someone looking hard will see them. There are places in your case a thief might miss, too, such as inside a bow tube. You might even want to add a reward statement.

4. Make a visual record of your violin and bow. If they were stolen tomorrow, would you be able to describe them accurately, so that someone else could recognize them? Make a file that contains detailed descriptions and clear photographs, and keep it in a safe place.

5. Get enough insurance and keep it up to date. It may seem expensive, but it's nothing compared to the price of replacing your violin and bow. You may think that your homeowner's policy will cover you, but the maximum payout may be too low, and if you use your instrument professionally it may not be covered at all. The ins and outs of instrument insurance can be convoluted, so read up on it and shop around. Some musical organizations offer group rates to members; it may be worth an annual fee just for the great deal they offer on insurance. Also, remember to get your instrument reappraised from time to time. Otherwise, you could find out too late that your policy won't pay for a comparable instrument because appreciation has left you behind.

6. In the event of theft, act quickly and spread your net wide. Chances are that the person who stole your violin isn't planning on playing it himself. He'll try to unload it as soon as possible for quick cash. The faster you get the word out, the more likely someone will recognize your instrument when it shows up in the hands of someone with a fishy story. After you call the police, start contacting music stores, violin dealers, and pawnshops. Visit in person if you can; store employees will be more willing to help and more likely to remember you later. Also, remember that the thief may figure he's safer dumping the instrument in a different town. Look up all the likely buyers within a 100-mile radius and call them as soon as possible. Get the word out to other players; they may see or hear something useful.

7. Make up a flyer. This is where the description and photographs come in handy. Add an explanation of when and how the instrument was stolen, plus the police case number and reward information (if any), and start distributing copies. Follow up all those phone calls to shops and dealers with a flyer in the mail. Distribute them wherever you can. Ask stores to post them prominently.

8. Check the local classified ads. It sounds incredible, but thieves actually have been known to advertise stolen goods in the local paper. If you were out of town when your instrument was taken, ask a friend or colleague in that location to keep an eye out for you.

9. Advertise on the Web. This can be quite inexpensive or even free, and it will reach a very wide audience. Sites to consider include www.stringsmagazine.com, which offers a free public forum; www.sdlmusic.com/hml/stolen.htm; and Maestronet, which offers a searchable on-line database (www.maestronet.com/stolen.html)

You can't chain your fiddle to your wrist, but there are several commonsense rules that can prevent you from losing your violin to theft.

INSURERS

A number of companies specialize in musical-instrument insurance and can help you find the right policy. Here are a few:

British Reserve Insurance Co Ltd
Musical Instruments Dept
Cornhill House
6 Vale Ave.
Tunbridge Wells
Kent, TN1 1EH
0870 2400 303
Fax: 0870 1600 304
Email: bric@cornhill.co.uk
www.britishreserve.co.uk

E & L Insurance
Thorpe Underwood Hall
Ouseburn
York, YO26 9SZ
01423 333000
Fax: 0870 7423810
remember@compuserve.com
www.EandL.co.uk

Hibernian Violins
67 SomersRd
Malvern
Worcs, WR14 1JA
Tel/Fax: 01684 562947

N W Brown Music Division
Richmond House
16-20 Regent St.
Cambridge, CB2 1DB
01223 357131
Fax: 01223 353705
music@nwbrown.co.uk

Musicians Insurance Services
312 High St.
Harlington
Hayes
Middlesex, UB3 BT
0208 564 8181
Fax:0208 564 9063
tlc@bryanjames.co.uk

Bloomfield and Associates
L4, 501 La Trobe St.
Melbourne 30000
9602 41 78
info@mackenzieross.com

Carrington Whittaker Insurance Brokers
Pty Ltd
1216 President Avenue
Caringbah NSW 2229
PO Box 504
Caringbah NSW 1495
toll-free: 1800 244350
(02) 9525 6877
fax: (02) 9526 2667
dennis.whittaker@apfs.com.au

Marsh Pty Ltd
Level 17
45 Pire Street
Adelaide SA
PO Box 2637
Adelaide SA 5001
toll-free: 1800 882317
(08)8211 7655
fax:(08) 8211 8785

State Insurance Ltd
1 Willis Street
PO Box 3233
Wellington
New Zealand
toll-free: 0800 802424
(04)4969600
fax: (04) 471 494 2764

of stolen stringed instruments and bows. For $50, Maestronet will scan your photograph and create an on-line listing that will run for the balance of the calendar year. The theft report will also be circulated to dealers and subscribers of Maestronet's stolen-instruments mailing list.

To sum up: when it comes to protecting your instrument, learn to be vigilant and take a little trouble beforehand to save yourself a lot of trouble later. If you do become a victim of theft, act quickly but be patient and persistent. And if the worst does happen and the instrument is gone for good, at least you'll know you did everything possible to get it back—and be able to buy a reasonable replacement with the insurance money.

MAINTAINING YOUR BOW'S CONDITION AND VALUE

by Mark R. Reindorf

When dealers, appraisers, and collectors assess the value of a bow, they consider the skill and reputation of the maker, the bow's current physical condition, and its playing or handling characteristics. While there is nothing you can do to change your bow's provenance, you can do a lot to maintain its condition.

An important consideration is whether the maker's intentions have been honored. Evaluators are concerned with the aesthetic integrity of the bow. Has any part been reformed or reshaped? Have any parts been repaired or replaced? Has the physical integrity of the bow been weakened through wear, cracks, breaks, or other damage? Expert appraisers usually express the impact of each change as a percentage of the current value of an actual or hypothetical perfect specimen built by the same maker.

Different problems have differing impacts on the bow's overall worth. For example, any change to the form of the bow shaft—the carving, tapering, placement of head or butt mortises, and cambering—seriously diminishes the value of the bow. Other cosmetic defects, such as scratches, nicks, bumps, burns, and knots at stress points, detract from overall appearance and value. But any major repair to the stick—a graft, splice, or repaired head—radically diminishes the bow's value.

This Nürnberger bow is showing signs of wear in its original tinsel-wrap winding.

WHERE YOUR BOW SHOWS THE MOST WEAR, AND WHY

Even a lovingly protected bow will show signs of wear if it is being used. The most prominent area of wear is the handle, and severe handle wear can diminish the value of an otherwise well-preserved bow by up to 35 percent. You can protect the handle area from excessive wear with a covering of thin leather or similar material. This will extend the life of the bow. Wear can also be considerable in the thumb area, especially on cello bows, and can reduce the bow's value by as much as a third. Replace the leather thumb grip as soon as it shows signs of wear, to prevent the stick from getting worn. These kinds of wear are often disguised with clear or colored epoxy resin. While this gives the illusion of fresh facets and a crisp octagon, the underlying damage is merely camouflaged.

The screw button is another point of wear. Over time, it can damage the butt end of the stick enough to require a bushing (an insertion of a small tubular piece of pernambuco to replace severely worn wood surrounding the screwbutton shaft). If skillfully installed, the bushing has no serious effect on the bow's overall value. But a

bushing added to reinforce a longitudinal crack will subtract at least ten percent from the bow's value—even though the original structural strength of the bow may have been restored.

The head of the bow is quite delicate, especially the extreme tip. Even though it's protected by an ivory plate, this tip can become cracked or split and require repair. Such damage can diminish a bow's value by about ten percent. Damage to the ridge, chamfer, and cheek contours, whether in the form of file marks, scratches, or dents, are not structural weaknesses. But they can take up to ten percent of a bow's value away for aesthetic reasons alone. A crack in the mortise area—where the block for holding the hair is inserted—is more severe, especially if the cheeks are split. Damage here will decrease value by at least 25 percent.

It is not unusual to find a bow shaft that has become slightly twisted, so that the frog is no longer perfectly aligned with the head. With an extremely valuable bow, it is considered imprudent to apply heat and lateral force sufficient to remove the twist, since a fracture or split might occur. In such a case, the frog is often readjusted on the stick to pro-

An 1875 Tubbs bow showing cracks in the frog and a worn grip.

duce a better alignment with the head. If properly done, this repair has only minimal effect on the bow's value.

The frog accounts for roughly 33 percent of the value of a bow by a major maker. The adjuster alone can account for 10 percent of the value. Of the frog's various silver parts, the most abused is generally the

The head of the bow is quite delicate, especially the extreme tip.

ferrule. Over years—not only decades but sometimes centuries—this small yet critical part is often squeezed, bent, split, scratched, and otherwise mistreated. Because accumulated rosin, dirt, and perspiration can greatly hinder the removal of the ferrule for rehairing, some damage is virtually inevitable. Bows entrusted to competent and qualified repairers, of course, show minimal damage and wear to this and other delicate parts of the frog.

The silver rings of the screw button are another problem area. When the ebony core absorbs excessive moisture, it is apt to push out and split the rings. They must then be resoldered or, if badly damaged or thinned, replaced. The heel plate and back plate (some bows have only one silver plate in this area, bent at a right angle and usually affixed with one or more small metal pins) are not subject to the same forces as the ferrule and screw button, but are often carelessly scratched or banged. Finally, the silver rings encircling the pearl eyes in bows by such makers as Sartory, Fétique, Ouchard, and Thomassin are quite thin and thus fragile. They can split, bend, and even occasionally fall out.

REPAIRS THAT CAN IMPROVE YOUR BOW'S WORTH

Just as certain skillful repairs to the stick will only minimally affect value, there are repairs to the frog and screw button mechanism that can do much to preserve the general condition of the bow. The insertion of a cheval is fairly common. Here, an ebony piece is joined to the part of the frog that meets the stick, replacing a worn or splintered surface. Replacing the ebony center of the button when the old ebony core is split or severely worn down, or the pearl eyes and slides when the originals have been worn or eaten away by perspiration, minimally affects value. And when a bow is in a state of continual service, a bottom slide may be inserted (even when not included by the original maker) to lessen wear on the frog.

There are many ways that you can protect your bow between maintenance visits to the shop or rehairer. Always protect the bow from impact or shock, and be careful not to drop it or bang the head. Keep the bow away from extreme heat, as is found in a closed car in bright sunshine, which could cause warping or twisting. Loosen the hair when you're not using the bow. Moving a taut bow from a humid climate to one that is extremely dry could actually snap the bow. Avoid exposing the bow to the harsh, abrasive pressure of fingernails by keeping nails short. Keep the bow clean, wiping off excess rosin and any perspiration after each use. They have a corrosive effect on your bow. Finally, when it is time to take your bow in for some work, be sure to use only experienced, qualified repairers and rehairers.

HOW TO PACK A BOW

by Peg Baumgartel

At some point you may need to ship your bow for repair or appraisal, and it is important to know how to do this safely so that your bow will arrive in one piece instead of in splinters. Packing a bow is a simple process, as you will see, but be forewarned: there is always a risk of damage when shipping. By learning how to pack properly, however, you can greatly limit your risk.

You will find the procedure very similar to packing a crystal vase; as you wrap your bow in protective layers, the key words to remember are *center, suspend*, and *immobilize*. First, loosen your bow's hair. The tension *must* be off the bow before you put it in the case. Forgetting this step can result in a broken head. Next, place the bow in its case and tuck foam rubber around the head and frog to immobilize the bow. You do not want your bow to move around in its case during transit—if the box is dropped and the bow shifts, the head could break. If you are using a PVC case, wrap the bow in bubble wrap and tape the ends shut before inserting it into the case. Stuff the PVC caps with more bubble wrap or foam rubber and tape the end caps to the PVC pipe.

Now it's time to pack the case inside a box. Your approach will vary depending on the shape of the box you're using. If your box is triangular, put several inches of bubble wrap or foam rubber in the bottom of it. Place your bow case in the center of the box and make sure you cannot push it to the bottom of the box. Fill in around the bow case with packing peanuts and tamp down firmly so they won't shift in transit and fail to protect your bow. Another option is to wrap many layers of bubble wrap around your bow case and tape it into place inside the box. To fill in the last few inches at the top of the box, lay down layers of bubble wrap or foam rubber.

If your box is rectangular, put several inches of packing peanuts in the bottom of the box, followed by a layer of bubble wrap that covers the length and width of the

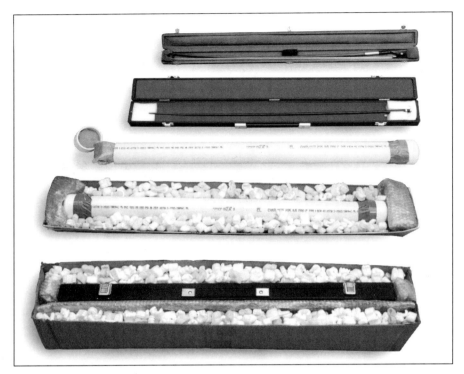

Safe ways to ship your bow (from top to bottom): a bow case for a single bow, a pool-cue case used as a bow case, a homemade case made from PVC pipe, and a PVC pipe and commercial case properly packed in shipping boxes.

box. Center your bow case in the box and surround the ends and sides with bubble wrap or foam rubber to prevent the case from shifting inside the box. Continue filling with packing peanuts until you reach the top of the box.

Close up the box, but before you seal the end with packing tape, shake the box gently to make sure that the bow case is centered, suspended, and immobilized. If the box flaps collapse inward when you close them, you need to add more peanuts. Use packing tape over the seams of the box even if they are preglued. Seal the box, place "fragile" stickers on all sides of the box, and complete your shipping label.

That's it! You've packed your bow like a professional.

UNDERSTAND
COMMON
REPAIRS

REPAIRING CRACKS

by James N. McKean

The strap on your case breaks, and your instrument tumbles to the ground with a sickening bump. Your heart in your mouth, you pick it up and open it, only to find what you had feared most: the jagged white line of a fresh crack on the top of your violin. The good news is that the effect of a repair, even a serious one, is almost always undetectable. And not all changes are for the worse; after being repaired, an instrument can often work better than it did before it was damaged. How can this be? The answer is that not all instruments are set up to produce the best sound to begin with. Often, setting the damage to right offers the opportunity to correct mistakes in the way the instrument was originally put together.

While it is true that the whole instrument vibrates when you play, some parts are more important than others. The top, for example, contributes much more to the sound than, say, the scroll or the lower block, and the center of the top is working much more than the outer flanks. So damage and subsequent repair are more likely to alter the sound and response of your instrument when they occur in these more active areas. Not by coincidence, the areas that vibrate more also tend to be where more tension is exerted. The additional strain means that more reinforcement is required to ensure that the repairs last—and more reinforcement means more likelihood that the sound or response of your instrument will be altered when you get it back.

WHERE AND WHY CRACKS APPEAR

Cracks are the most common form of damage. The top and back of your instrument are, comparatively speaking, quite thin. For a violin, standard thicknesses of the plates range from 2.5 mm. to 3 or 4.5 mm. in the center. That's not much, considering the amount of force exerted on the instrument when it is strung up and played, but it allows for a delicate balance. The plates have to be strong enough to withstand indefinitely the tremendous pressure exerted on them without seriously deforming, but flexible enough to provide the mobility and resonance that creates the sound. In addition, when an arch is carved out of the wood it creates inequalities of strength, and the weaker areas are just where the most strength is needed.

FIXING THE CRACK

When a crack does open up, the only proper way to repair it is to take the top off the instrument first, although unfortunately not all instruments are worth the expense and time of doing this. The reasons for having the top off are twofold. It is of paramount importance for the crack to be perfectly flush when it is glued, and the only way to achieve this is by using clamps down the entire length of the crack. The other reason is to reinforce the crack. Gluing the surface of the crack itself is not enough to insure that it will not separate again, so small pieces of wood called studs are carefully fitted over the underside of the crack, where they act as permanent sutures. The fear of changing the instrument's sound when repairing cracks is real,

Clamps are placed along the entire length of a crack to ensure that it is properly glued.

but it is, of course, possible to minimize the effect. One method that is actually quite old but coming back into vogue involves the use of parchment studs rather than wood. Parchment holds the wood together as effectively as wood, but it's more flexible.

Once the crack is properly glued and reinforced, it must be retouched so that the bare wood is properly sealed and the appearance of the damage is blended with the surrounding area. A common misconception among musicians is that a visible crack is a badly repaired one. Older cracks tend to show and can even turn black with age, since the glue that is used is hydroscopic—it absorbs moisture out of the air and, with it, ambient dirt. The glue itself can also be discolored by the acid naturally found in wood. These dark cracks can still be holding fine; and even if they move a bit, it doesn't necessarily mean that they must be redone. Remember, the whole instrument is moving and vibrating while you're playing it.

A crack can also show if the natural patina of the old varnish has been preserved, for it will have the irregularities of a lifetime of wear; a newly retouched crack will be more even and shiny. Unfortunately, the mania for invisible cracks means that much unnecessary retouching is done. Be aware that the purity of the varnish of an antique

A reinforced bass bar sets with clamps in place to prevent slipping.

instrument is a large part of its value, and that the larger world views such overvarnishing and polishing as vandalism. If it becomes necessary to have a crack repaired on your instrument, be sure that the shop you intend to patronize does not have a reckless hand with the brush.

WHEN NOT TO REPAIR A CRACK

There are some cracks that do need to be securely repaired, and two of these are soundpost and bass-bar cracks. These parts must be solid because they carry a good part of the stress exerted on an instrument. Even the slightest crack in the soundpost area will very likely travel if it is not properly glued and reinforced, and a simple stud won't hold it. The proper repair is a patch, a new piece of wood inlaid into the old and then feathered to the original thickness; it is actually replacing old wood with new.

Even the slightest crack in the soundpost area will very likely travel if it is not properly glued and reinforced.

When properly glued, a repaired crack itself will have virtually no effect on the sound and response of your instrument. Hide glue is enormously strong; a glue joint, in fact, will be stronger than the wood surrounding it. Vibration will not be affected, as your instrument already has one (and usually two) "cracks" that run from one end of the plate to the other: the center joints of the top and the back, if it's a two-piece back. The crack won't affect the sound, either, as there is absolutely no difference in sound between a one-piece and a two-piece back.

What *can* affect the sound, sometimes dramatically, is the reinforcement that must be done to ensure that the crack doesn't reopen. Let's say that the crack is off to the side—in the lower bout of the top or back. Little reinforcement is needed, since there is almost no stress in this area. It's provided only to counteract the future effects of weather, so the crack won't reopen as the plate shrinks and expands with the changing seasons. When a spruce stud or parchment repair has been properly executed, a repairman should be able to bend the top and not feel any difference in the flex over the repaired area.

Visible cracks usually are of no more than aesthetic concern, unless in the areas of highest stress. On the ribs, for example, an open crack is not even worth talking about as long as it has a reinforcement to keep it from traveling. If it doesn't affect the structural stability and making it "go away" will adversely affect the sound, why do it? Besides, such efforts are very expensive and can, ironically, result in damage to the original varnish surrounding the crack, thus negatively affecting sound and value.

Toast usually lands jelly-side down, and when an instrument lands it's very seldom the unimportant areas that are damaged. Mostly it's in the center, the area that suffers the most strain and contributes most to the vibration. Cracks caused by accidents frequently occur around the soundholes or over the soundpost or bass bar. Makers know the soundholes as the "hinges" of the instrument, and they compensate by leaving the wood around the soundhole extra thick. When a crack does appear, though, the reinforcement must be handled differently and presents a greater chance that the sound and, more important, the response will be altered. The reinforcement must be made larger, which often stiffens the top. Again, though, this is not necessarily a bad thing; many older instruments have reinforcements around the soundholes even though there are no cracks, because they improve the response and add more focus and power to the sound.

This is where the repairer must be sensitive to the expectations and taste of the player. After all, it's your instrument; and while the numbers might be wrong and the sound (to the repairer) uninspired, or lacking in punch, to you it might be velvety, dark, and quick to respond. So if you are in need of a major repair and the repairer starts talking about correcting things that are wrong, be sure that he fully understands the tonal consequences of what he proposes and that he has clearly explained them to you.

Reinforcing a bass-bar crack requires removing the bar, adding studs over the crack, and fitting and gluing a new bar over the studs. No matter how this is done, the result will be a changed instrument. Even a new bar identical to the one removed

> **EXERCISE CAUTION**
>
> Remember that the repairer often makes a living doing repairs. The more extensive they are, the more money the repairer makes. A reputable shop will always act conservatively; the better ones are usually swamped with work, anyway. Be extremely cautious if the repairer asks if you have insurance before giving you an estimate, or if a simple repair escalates into a major restoration. The words to watch out for are, "While we have it open. . . ." Remember, too, anyone can set himself up as an expert. So don't just run to the nearest shop; you'll die of shock at the results of a bad job a lot sooner than the instrument will from the accident.

will result in a different instrument, at least until it plays in. A good repairman, how-ever, will know how to balance the demands of the reinforcing studs and the bar to approximate the amount of support the old bar gave you—and, more than that, improve it if you found it lacking.

Many times accidents cause the neck to come out of the instrument. If it is reset with exactly the same measurements, then once the instrument settles down, it will be just as it was. If anything is changed, though, the sound will be altered, since the way the neck is set governs the tension on the instrument. So if the repairer says that this is an excellent opportunity to replace the fingerboard or give you more clearance with the bow in the c-bouts, alarm bells should go off. If the proposed work will affect the sound, think carefully before proceeding, because once it's done it cannot be undone.

A JOB WELL DONE

When the job is finally done and you get the instrument back, you will want to try it out immediately. Before you do, remember that any instrument that has not been played needs to be "woken up" and played in. This is true even if it has just had the strings taken off for a thorough cleaning. On the other hand, don't be afraid to go back for adjustments if after a week or so the sound hasn't begun to return to what you remember.

So if the worst happens to you and a visit to the repair shop is unavoidable, take solace in the fact that the chances are very good that the worst damage will be to your investment and your own feelings of equanimity. Insurance should compensate for the first, and you can recover from the second. Your instrument's acoustics will most likely end up pretty much as they were before. An instrument is remarkably durable and, if at all old, has probably been through it all before. Your only task is to get it into the right hands, make sure that you are told just what will be done to bring it back to life, and then relax.

AGING AND ITS EFFECTS ON YOUR VIOLIN

by James N. McKean

The varnish on your violin is one of the most important factors in its sound and value, and the fresher it is, the better. The reason for this is that varnish is applied not just to protect the wood; it also contributes to the individual character of the sound. Violin varnishes vary widely in their composition and the way they age. They are designed to be fragile and are expected to wear; the tougher a varnish is, the more it restricts the vibration of the wood. Often what appears to be damage might in fact be no more than the normal aging of a varnish film.

Aside from the usual wear, heat and dryness can damage an instrument, by causing either the glue to fail, cracks to develop, or the varnish to be degraded. Just leaving the violin under the direct sun—even in its case—can cause the varnish to bubble and flake off. If the damage on your instrument goes beyond normal aging, you may need to have the instrument's condition evaluated. Restoring the varnish is

A worn upper bout.

a delicate process that requires experience and care to preserve as much of what is left of the original as possible.

Keep in mind that nicks and scratches happen all the time, and you can console yourself with the thought that they always look a lot worse than they are. They can be filled and retouched so that they are, at worst, hardly visible. Under no circumstances try to take care of this on your own—you will quickly find a disaster on your hands, one that will be much harder for a repairer to put right (and therefore expensive, too). The best you can do is keep the area clean. Don't touch it, since oils and dirt from your finger will be absorbed by the bare wood. And never put tape over the damaged area to protect it—since the varnish is fragile it's almost impossible to get the tape off without causing further damage to the surrounding areas.

Scrapes and scratches are most noticeable on new instruments, where they really stand out. They can be retouched, but it is best just to relax and let them accumulate; after all, it is the wear that contributes to the beauty and allure of older violins. They add character, and they are an inevitable part of aging. Retouching on old instruments gets to be a problem when too much of it is done. This is a state of affairs that is becoming all too common; current taste calls for an evened-out look that requires extensive over-varnishing and polishing, in the process destroying the texture and patina of great old varnish. The result is a glassy, monochromatic finish that robs the instrument of its warmth and individuality. If you are lucky enough to have a fine old instrument, do not let an overzealous repairer sell you on the idea that it must be without imperfections and have a high shine. Once it has reached that stage, it can never go back, and you will have sacrificed one of the most valuable aspects of your instrument.

Generally, the value of the instrument will determine whether it warrants the expense and time that would be involved in restoration. Any such evaluation—not only of the extent of the damage and the proper approach to restoring the varnish, but especially the instrument's overall value—must be done with the instrument in hand. Other possible damage to the instrument, varnish aside, is also something that can be assessed only by a qualified repairer. When showing your instrument to a repairer, you won't be charged for a preliminary evaluation—a quick yes or no, in other words—but do keep in mind that for any violin maker or repairer, time is money, so if you want more detailed information, be prepared to pay. Most repair shops do not charge for estimates of repair. To find someone in your area, you can consult the *British and International Music Yearbook* (Rhinegold Publishing, London) or try *Strings* magazine's *Resource Guide*, available as the latest October issue and also on-line at www.stringsmagazine.com.

LOCATING BUZZES

by James N. McKean

Buzzes are the bane of the musician's (and the repairer's) life. They might be caused by something as simple as a loose E tuner or as serious as an unglued patch on the inside of your instrument. The frustrating part is isolating the culprit: any one of the myriad parts of the instrument—to say nothing of its repairs—could be the cause. Complicating matters further is the fact that some buzzes will appear only under certain conditions—and almost never when you take your instrument in to the repair shop for evaluation. Oftentimes there can be more than one buzz going on at a

Open bouts are a common contributor to instrument buzzes.

time; the trick is to identify the one causing the worst trouble and then find its source. The only way to do this is to eliminate the suspects one by one, and this can be a time-consuming and therefore costly job.

Buzzes almost always sound as though they are coming from the left f-hole, which is why people commonly blame them on a loose bass bar. This is almost never the cause. When you begin the search—and you should look as much as you can before you head to the shop—check the strings, since they will begin to buzz as their windings loosen. Next, check for open bouts and then for anything loose in the setup, something like a loose tuner in the tailpiece or a chin rest that isn't completely tight, or even (not uncommonly) the pegs. If you haven't found the cause by this time, you will probably have to seek help at a professional shop. Many shops, by the way, will refuse to search out buzzes in an instrument that was purchased elsewhere.

The most frequent cause of buzzing is purfling that has come unglued and is rattling in its channel, particularly on the top around the c-bouts. This can be the result of poor clamping when an open bout was being glued. The problem can be taken care of, but the chances are very good that it will recur at some point. Any cracks will also have to be checked to see if they are open or if their reinforcements inside have come loose, especially if they are near the bass bar.

The decision to continue the search inside the instrument is one taken only as a last resort, because it means removing the top, which involves considerable time and expense. Anything that is loose on the inside could be the cause of the problem, and all the old repairs will have to be checked minutely and possibly redone. Since the instrument resonates as a box, you can't know for sure that the problem has been solved until you've glued the top back on. Remember, the whole purpose of your instrument is to act as an amplifier—the strings can't be heard by themselves. But it will amplify everything, including buzzes, so something that is inaudible when you tap a part by itself can suddenly come alive when the box is back together and resonating. A violin has more than 120 separate pieces of wood that have been bent, joined, and glued together with hide glue; some are under pressure, and all are subject to constant vibration. So it's not surprising that sometimes a piece comes loose.

While a buzz might be found and cured, oftentimes it will return, no matter how much time, effort, and money have gone into tracking it down. Frustrating as buzzes are—and they can be enormously so—the only consolation is that the audience can't hear any but the very worst, and those are the ones that can almost always be found.

ADJUSTING THE SOUNDPOST

by James N. McKean

If your soundpost is too short, it might fall down when you take the string pressure off your instrument. This sometimes happens when the weather suddenly turns cold and dry—you'll open the case only to discover that the pegs have all come loose (the wood in the pegbox and pegs shrinks from the drop in moisture). If the post does fall over, you will need to have a longer one fitted.

Some makers and repairers will fit a soundpost that is too long in an effort to boost the instrument's power and edge. Initially, it will have the desired effect, but within days it will wear off as the instrument stretches to accommodate the longer post. Over time, a too-long post can cause serious damage, distorting the arching or even opening a crack. Also beware the common misconception that instruments need soundposts of different lengths for summer and winter.

Over time, a soundpost that is too long can damage your violin's top.

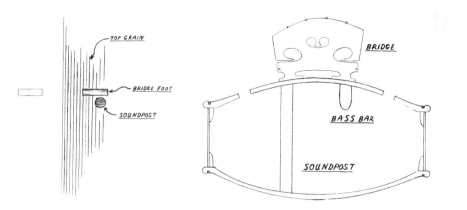

TOP GRAIN

BRIDGE FOOT

SOUNDPOST

BRIDGE

BASS BAR

SOUNDPOST

The soundpost as seen from above (left) and an inside view of the soundpost (right).

Soundposts do occasionally need adjusting, however—a process steeped in mystery. Anyone who has spent time around violins knows that there is a cult of the adjustment, a sort of acoustic juju with which some people are reputed to be endowed. It does take a certain touch, but it isn't much of a mystery.

Take a quick look at the diagram above, which shows the position of the soundpost as viewed from above. It does not sit directly under the bridge foot; rather, it is slightly behind it, and slightly to the inside. Both of these distances are changed when the post is adjusted. By moving the post in or out—to the left or right on the diagram—the rocking motion of the bridge is affected. Moving it out makes it stiffer (much as spreading your feet steadies your stance), which throws more of the rocking to the bass bar and affects the balance of the sound of the strings. Moving the post closer or further from the entire bridge—up or down on the diagram—also changes the amount of time it takes the sound waves to reach the back, thus affecting the focus or depth of the sound. As slight as it is, this phase delay between the resonance of the top and the back contributes to the complexity of the violin's overtones.

By moving the post in these two directions, the instrument's response and tone quality can be fine-tuned. An experienced adjuster can tell what needs to be done by listening and watching as you play. Anything you can put into words will also help, and you shouldn't feel shy about expressing what it is that is troubling you about the way your instrument is responding. The exact vocabulary isn't important, although there is a lexicon for the adjusting process; *sluggish, nasal, covered, too dark,* and *metallic* are a few of the terms commonly used.

The most important thing to remember about the adjustment of your instrument is that it cannot be optimal all the time. Any halfway decent violin is built to be responsive, to the weather and the seasons as much as to the pressure of the bow. As an amplifier, the instrument amplifies your mood as well as the sound of the strings. If you're having an off day, the chances are excellent that your instrument will, too. Avoid the temptation to have the instrument adjusted for every variation you feel or hear in its response. The French have it right: the soundpost is like the soul, best nourished by being least troubled.

REFERENCE

A COMPLETE VIOLIN GLOSSARY

by James N. McKean

Adjust To move the soundpost, using a soundpost setter, in order to balance the response of the strings. Although the procedure looks simple, you should not try it yourself or you might cause serious damage.

Arch The curve of the back and the top. Contrary to popular belief, the wood is carved, not bent, to achieve this effect. The raw blanks for the top and back are shaped like peaked rooftops. The arch is roughed out with a gouge, refined with specially designed thumb planes, and finished with a steel scraper to make a perfect curve. The shape of the arch, its fullness and height, is one of the primary factors determining the sound of an instrument.

Bass bar A strip of spruce fitted and glued to the inside of the violin's top under the bass foot of the bridge. The bass bar supports the top and distributes the vibrations. Its shape and fit are critical to the response and power of your instrument.

Bearclaw Also known as *hazel,* it's the curlicue figure found in the wood of some tops and backs. The effect may be caused by a virus that affected the growing tree, or it might be genetic, like curly hair. Bearclaw does not affect an instrument's sound as long as there isn't too much of it.

Bee sting The point where the purfling meets in the violin's corners. The outside black strips are cut so that they extend to a fine point. The Amatis were masters at cutting these.

Belly The *top.* An older term more commonly used in England than in the U.S.

Blocks Chunks of willow or spruce inside your instrument (one at each end and one in each corner for a total of six) that reinforce the joints where the ribs meet and help distribute the stress on the neck and the saddle.

Book-match Most violin backs and almost all tops are made of two pieces of wood, sawn or split from a single billet and then opened up like a book and joined in the middle.

Bout The big upper or lower curve of an instrument's outline. An open bout is a seam that has come unglued between a rib and the top or back. See *c-bout.*

Bridge A maple support that holds the strings up and transmits their vibration to the instrument. The bridge must be fitted to the individual instrument and is held in place by the pressure of the strings. It has a decided effect on sound and response. The shape of the bridge's crown—the curve of its top—determines the ease of string crossing.

Bushing The dowel used to fill a peg hole or endpin hole that has gotten too large from wear. The hole is filled, retouched, and then redrilled, and the peg or endpin refit. It's a standard procedure that shouldn't affect the value of the instrument if done properly.

Button 1. A half moon–shaped piece of wood the size of the upper joint of your thumb that extends from the top of the back and covers the neck heel. Its humble size belies its critical role in anchoring the neck. A detached button spells big trouble, because it indicates that the neck is no longer securely set. If the button is worn and becomes too small, an ebony crown is often fitted to restore it to its proper size. See *double.* 2. The extension at the end of the bow by which you adjust the length of the hair. Having the original one affects the value of your bow. See *mounting.* It is attached to the screw and occasionally comes adrift, at which point it has to reattached. Let the bow maker do this. See *nut.*

Camber The curve in the bow stick. In a very delicate and precise operation, the maker bends the bow, having heated it over a flame. The shape and distribution of the camber are critical to your bow's performance, and altering them is an art.

C-bout The curve in an instrument's outline that makes up its waist.

Chamfer The 45-degree bevel that breaks the sharp edge on the scroll. The way it's done is a signature of a maker's style; the brothers Amati hardly used one, while Storioni whacked it out—each in keeping with the general feel of their instruments.

Channel The reverse curve over the instrument's purfling where the arch rises to meet the edge. The depth and extent of the channel play a critical role in determining the sound and response of the instrument. The deeper it is, the more flexible the plate is, yielding a faster response but not as much resistance. As the instrument evolved, the channel gradually became less and less deep as makers strove to create instruments with greater power.

Collar The ebony or ivory ring between the shaft and head of the peg. Loose collars often cause buzzing.

Comb The hollowing, with a ridge in the middle, that runs from the back of the scroll to the front of the volute. Stradivari's was distinctive and elegant, flattening in the middle and achieving a wonderfully sculptural effect.

Corner The place where the bouts converge—four on the back, four on the top. They present a paradox, for the better they are aesthetically, the more of an irritant they are to the player. Long, graceful corners tend to fall victim to exuberant bowing, because the frog will catch them and pull them off. So why do makers go on making them? Because they are so beautiful.

Double To repair a detached button by thinning it and grafting on new wood. See *button*.

Dovetail The joint by which the neck is attached to the body of the instrument.

Dress To plane the fingerboard and remove irregularities worn into it through use. See *fingerboard*.

Ear We could debate whether every musician (or instrument maker) has one, but every violin should. It's the very outer part—the smallest turn, the little circle—on the volute.

Ebony The tropical hardwood used for the fingerboard and some fittings, chosen because it is so dense and resistant to wear.

Edge The perimeter of the top or back—the part outside the purfling that overhangs the rib structure. The way it's rounded is another signature of the maker.

Endbutton The little wooden knob fitted into a hole in the lower ribs, over which the tailgut passes.

Eye The small pearl circle inlaid into the sides of the frog. The size and position are characteristic of the maker's work. When a plain eye is used, the button is almost always a sandwich of metal-ebony-metal. The Parisian eye is a more elaborate inlay in the side of the frog, with a metal circle around the pearl dot. If this is used, the button is always solid metal of a type to match the rest of the mounting. Vuillaume was famous for his optical lens eyes—held up to the light, you can see a photographic image inside the frog. Some makers, usually German, used silver eyes; some used nothing at all, leaving the frog unadorned. As pearl is susceptible to wear, the eyes occasionally have to be replaced.

Eyelet See *screw.*

Faceplate See *tip.*

Ferrule The small semicircle of metal covering the protruding tongue of the frog where the hair goes in. See *mounting.*

F-hole The soundhole of the instrument, so called because of its shape. The placement and cut of the f-holes are crucial to the sound of the instrument because they determine the way the top flexes as the instrument is played. Cut entirely with a knife, they are a test of the maker's eye and skill.

F-stop The distance from the top edge, next to the neck, to the notches of the f-hole, which determines the total string length. The neck length is proportional to the f-stop, so that when you shift, you land in the right position. When musicians feel that an instrument is too large, usually what they mean is that the f-stop (and thus the string length, and the stretch between notes) is too long.

Fiddle A *violin,* whether it's used to play classical, bluegrass, jazz, or any other kind of music. Everybody, from musicians to fine-instrument dealers, uses the term at least occasionally, so don't let unfounded fears about the Snob Police affect your own choice of vocabulary.

Figure The pattern in the wood of the back, ribs, and scroll. It is not wood grain, but patterns made by the undulation of the grain as the tree grows. You see it because the wood fibers, due to their changing direction, absorb differing amounts of varnish, which then reflect and diffract the light hitting them.

Filler See *ground.*

Fine tuner See *tuner.*

Fingerboard The ebony surface under the strings. Each fingerboard is individually fitted to the instrument. Its surface is arched to mimic the arch of the bridge, although a cello fingerboard has a flat table under the C string that provides a better surface for fingering the thicker string. See *dress, scoop.*

Fittings The pegs, tailpiece, endbutton or endpin, and chin rest. Most are made of ebony, but rosewood, boxwood, and mountain mahogany are also used. They might be, but usually aren't, original to an older instrument.

Flame See *figure*.

Fleck See *mirror*.

French polish A high-gloss varnish that amalgamates with an instrument's original varnish, irreversibly debasing its patina and changing its acoustical effects.

Frog The sliding part to which the lower end of the hair is attached. It's held in place by the screw and eyelet, and usually has a metal liner on the surface that slides along the bow stick. Adjusting it tightens or loosens the hair. Most frequently of ebony, ivory and tortoiseshell were also used historically on finer bows. As the use of both materials is now banned, you should be very careful about traveling with a bow made with them, as they stand an excellent chance of being seized and destroyed by customs agents. Having the original frog is very important to the value of your bow. If you have a rare or expensive bow, or one that does not have a liner, consider having a replacement made for everyday use to preserve the original.

Graduation The variations in thickness of the top and back. The top is left thicker around the f-holes and the upper and lower blocks; the back is thicker in the center, gradually thinning toward the flanks. The graduation of the plates is a determining factor in sound and response. See *regraduation*.

Grain The annular rings of the tree; two new ones, for winter and summer, accrue every year. When viewed on a violin, the grain must be as straight and true as possible.

Ground Also called the undercoat, sealer, or filler, it's what goes on the wood first when applying the finish. The wood of a raw violin is tremendously absorbent, so what is applied first will soak in deeply and affect the way the wood vibrates and thus the sound of the finished instrument. Not necessarily a varnish, the filler each maker uses is something he or she holds strong views on but will rarely, if ever, discuss. Old Cremonese and Venetian instruments, celebrated for their tonal superiority, feature an exceptionally beautiful ground, the composition of which is still largely unknown.

Grip The material, leather or lizardskin, wrapped around the lower end of the winding for your thumb and forefinger to rest against. It serves a dual role, as padding and protection for the lapping. Have it replaced the minute it wears through.

Hair Horsehair, from the tails. Musicians and bow makers all harbor a variety of beliefs as to what kind is best. It is either white or black—the white is often bleached, but this reduces its strength. Black hair is usually coarser and has a harder bite on the strings. The hair is rough, but it's the rosin that makes it grab the string.

Hardwood The back, sides, and neck of an instrument are always of hardwood: maple, poplar, or sometimes willow.

Hazel See *bearclaw*.

Head 1. The scroll. 2. The part at the upper end of the stick (on the bow) to which the hair is attached. The shape of the head is the most identifiable expression of the personality of the maker. They are usually in one of two shapes, either hatchet or swan (the latter being most commonly found on cello bows).

Hide glue What holds the instrument together, a gelatin glue made from cow hooves and hides. It is used because it's water soluble, which means that glue joints can be dissolved and taken apart for repair when necessary and for the simple reason that after a thousand years or so of invention, it's still the best and most versatile adhesive around.

Joint Each place where two pieces of wood meet and are glued. A clean joint is one that is holding well; an open joint is one that has failed. The center joint is where the two halves of the top or back are glued together.

Label The slip of paper glued inside the instrument's back, identifying the maker. Also called the sticker or ticket.

Lapping Also called *wrapping* or *winding*, it's the winding on the lower end of the stick to protect from the wear of your fingers. Traditional wrapping was either metal thread or whalebone. Whalebone being illegal, makers use synthetic (although many have a secret hoard of old culled and carefully cleaned whalebone lapping that they will reuse on the very best bows). Most makers now use solid metal wire for its durability and weight (silver or gold, to match the mounting; the winding is not technically a part of the mounting, since it isn't integral to the bow). It will eventually wear through, or one end will come unsoldered, and then it will have to be replaced.

Liner Found on all but the oldest bows, a metal plate on the top of the frog where it slides against the stick. It reinforces and protects the narrow flanges on each side of the top, which are very easily cracked. The manner in which it is attached is another clue as to the maker of the bow.

Lining The strips of wood glued to the inside of the rib structure to reinforce the joint where the plates meet the ribs. They can wear down after generations of regluing open bouts or be damaged by an impatient repairer with a dull gluing knife, at which point they have to be replaced. A bout that constantly opens might not have a lining adequate to hold the rib and plate together.

Maple The greatest of all woods in appearance, grain, resonance, and strength. The best comes from Bosnia.

Mirror Also called *fleck,* it's the medulary rays in maple that, under a great varnish, sparkle and reflect the light.

Mounting (Or simply *mount*) The metal used on the bow frog and button. Silver is the most frequently used, with gold found on finer bows (a myth, really; "more expensive" is more accurate). Gold, being heavier, will affect the weight and balance. There are different types of silver that help identify particular makers or schools; coin silver is the grade used, for its resistance to wear. Nickle is found on the cheapest bows, except those made between the wars, due to economic conditions in Europe at the time. Nickle mountings on fine bows are rare, for they are often replaced with silver.

Neck The part of the instrument with which you have most contact. The thickness, rounding, and finish must be exactly right. Like grammar or pitch, you only notice it when it's bad, but then it's as irritating as a stone in your shoe.

Neck graft A new neck that has replaced a broken or worn one and connects the violin with its original scroll.

Neck heel The vertical part of the neck where it is joined to the body, ending in the button. Also called the root.

Notches Also called *nicks,* these are the little knife cuts in the middle of the f-holes that indicate the location of the bridge.

Nut The ebony piece at the upper end of the fingerboard that supports the strings. The angle of the grooves that holds the strings is very important: if too steep, the strings will break; if too flat, they will sound false. See *button.*

Open bout See *bout.*

Overhang The projection of the edge over the rib structure. It allows the plates to fit on the ribs yet still expand and shrink with changes in the weather.

Overstand The distance from the top to the fingerboard where the neck is joined to the instrument. It is a vitally important measurement, for two reasons. First, the overstand will make a huge difference in your ability to shift comfortably into the upper positions. Second, the amount of pressure exerted on the top by the strings—and thus a large part of the sound and response—is a function of the overstand and the projection of the neck.

Patch A repair that involves removing original wood and replacing it with new, necessary in places where so much pressure is exerted that a crack will not hold if only glued and reinforced with studs. The most common are soundpost patches.

Peg The posts around which the strings are wound. Shaped to have precisely the same taper as the peg hole, the peg should turn and hold without having to be pushed in. If your pegs slip, they might need peg dope, a compound to be applied very sparingly.

Peg holes The four holes in the scroll where the pegs go. They must be perfectly round for the pegs to turn smoothly. Since peg dope will accumulate and harden, the peg holes have to be cleaned now and then. See *bushing.*

Pegbox The lower, functional part of the scroll that holds the pegs and strings.

Pernambuco Except for the very cheapest bows, the wood the stick is made from. An extremely strong and dense wood, it is only found in the valley of the Pernambuco River in Brazil. There is great concern about future sources of bow wood, since the existing stands of pernambuco have suffered from extensive deforestation, and the tree is perilously close to becoming extinct.

Pin In the classic method of construction, two small pins at the upper and lower ends of the plates were used to hold them in place while gluing. Made of wood, they are visible near the center joint by the purfling. Their precise location and size are characteristics that can be used to identify the work of a particular maker.

Pine English term for spruce.

Plates The top and back of the instrument.

Plug The small pieces of wood, two of them, that hold the hair in place inside the mortises in the head and frog. You can't see them; the upper one is covered by the hair, the lower one by the slide.

Projection The height of the neck at the bridge. Combined with the overstand and arching height, it gives a rough calculation of the angle of the strings over the bridge and affects the pressure that is exerted on the top. A higher projection results in more pressure. The projection varies with the weather. As humidity increases, the neck drops. A projection that is too low makes it difficult to bow without clobbering the c-bouts.

Purfling The three-piece strip that runs around the perimeter of the instrument. Almost always inlaid, purfling serves a dual purpose: aesthetically, it's like a picture frame, and functionally, it acts as a binder, preventing cracks from developing and traveling along the grain. The purfling is occasionally scratched or painted on. Purfling that has come loose in the groove is the most common source of buzzes.

Re-cambering If your bow is not playing as it once did, and a rehair doesn't solve the problem, it most likely needs recambering. The bow maker can tell with a glance at the stick, after watching you play a few notes.

Regraduation What amounts to a retrofit, in which the graduations of a violin are redone by someone other than the maker.

Rehair A verb or a noun; replacing the hank of hair on your bow. It's done when you've lost enough hair or it's old enough that it no longer grabs the string. A proper rehair will not have too much hair, just enough so there is a slight rounding on the edge of the flat ribbon. Too much hair, a common error, makes the bow unresponsive and difficult to handle.

Ribs The sides of the instrument. Usually of the same wood as the back, they are very thin and are bent to shape on a hot iron. Stradivari and other classical makers often lined their cello ribs with linen to reinforce them.

Root See *neck heel.*

Rosin When you slash a pine tree, you get sticky sap oozing out. It's refined into turpentine and colophony, commonly known as rosin. It's sticky; dance studios use it to keep the floors from getting too slippery. For a violinist, it comes in cakes, in a bewildering array of types and brands and costs. Light rosin is thought to be finer, dark rosin more coarse (as with the hair, this is basically an extension of deep mythological prejudices linking color and behavioral characteristics). Some even has flecks of gold in it. People will swear by one or the other, but when you get down to it, it's just rosin. Powdered on the bow, it all looks the same and pretty much acts the same. The main thing to keep in mind is to use it sparingly—it builds up fast, and then has the opposite effect, making the bow slip.

Saddle 1. The small piece of ebony at the lower end of the instrument, over which the tailgut passes. 2. The slight flattening of the arch of the top (seen when viewed from the side) that enhances its flexibility.

Scoop The slight hollowing of the fingerboard that prevents strings from buzzing. The scoop must be perfectly even throughout its length. Too much scoop will result in the strings feeling too high in the middle positions, create intonation problems, and (in cellos) make it more difficult to barre fifths.

Screw The frog is held in place by a small screw that extends inside the end of the stick and is turned by the button. The screw goes through a threaded eyelet, which is attached to the frog; you can see it if you unscrew the button all the way. The screw fits in a hole drilled through the butt end of the stick. When the hole wears, the screw will put undue pressure on the stick, eventually cracking it. The worn hole is bushed with a dowel of pernambuco and redrilled so the screw fits snugly. The threads of the screw can strip, as can the eyelet; you'll know this has happened when you try to tighten the bow and you adjust the button and nothing happens to the hair. Both can be replaced easily, and are rarely original.

Scroll The head of the instrument (and a good guide to the artistry of the maker).

Sealer See *ground*.

Setup Broadly speaking, this term refers to the way everything is put together to make the instrument sound the way it does. The important parts in setup are the bridge and soundpost, and the important measurements are the f-stop, neck length, overstand, and projection.

Shaft The tapered shank of the peg.

Side See *ribs*.

Snakewood A dense hardwood, often used for the sticks on Baroque bows instead of pernambuco.

Softwood See *spruce*.

Soundhole See *f-hole.*

Soundpost The dowel of spruce that is wedged in place inside the instrument just behind the treble foot of the bridge. It supports the top and transmits the sound-waves to the back. Moving the post will alter the balance, response, and focus of the sound. The post must fit the surface of the back and top as perfectly as possible to avoid damaging either. A crack that develops over the post is known as a soundpost crack.

Spruce The softwood used for the top. Engelmann spruce, the most widely used species, grows all over the world. Spruce has the highest strength-to-weight ratio of any natural material. See *pine.*

Stamp Instruments have labels, and bows have stamps to serve the same purpose of indentifiying the maker. But not always—most makers, even the most famous, sold their bows directly to a shop, which would stamp the bow with the shop name. Stamps are easily forged, and it takes the most expert eye to tell the real from the fake. If at all possible, have tape put over a stamp to protect it; they can wear away alarmingly fast.

Stick What you have in your hand when you take everything off the bow—hair, frog, etc. The stick can be octagonal or round; while makers and players have preferences, there is no difference in terms of value or playability.

Sticker See *label.*

String length The distance between the bridge and the nut, and the governing factor in the playability of an instrument. Too long, and the reach between notes becomes awkward; too short, and the strings lose the tension necessary for good response.

Stud A reinforcement glued over a crack on the inside of the instrument. It can be of either spruce or parchment, and if attached properly it is acoustically invisible. The studs act like sutures, holding the crack together as it vibrates and moves due to weather.

Table See *belly.*

Tailgut The piece of line that is attached to the tailpiece and looped around the end-button or endpin. Plastic cable is now used instead of gut. The tailgut can be adjusted so that the distance between the bridge and the tailpiece can be tuned for optimum resonance: the string length behind the bridge should be one-sixth of the playable string length.

Tailpiece What the strings are attached to at the lower end. Although usually of a wood that matches the pegs, tailpieces of metal or plastic are also commonly found on cellos and sometimes violas. The material and weight of the tailpiece affects the sound, although there is no correlation as to the effect. Heavier tailpieces don't always make a darker sound, for example.

Tenor extension The widening of the pegbox above the nut on cellos and some violas. Done for aesthetic as well as practical reasons, the width balances with the instrument and the length of the scroll, and it allows more room for the strings in the pegbox. This was particularly important when the instrument was developed and the strings, being of braided gut, were much thicker.

Thumb stop The distance from the top edge where the neck is set to the recurve where the neck turns into the neck root. It's where your thumb rests as you shift into higher positions.

Ticket See *label.*

Tip Also called the faceplate, the reinforcement glued onto the base of the bow head to prevent it from splitting due to the wedge inside that holds the hair in place. The tip is traditionally ivory, although since elephants are now an endangered species, horn or mastadon tusk is often used in its place (many bow makers have a stockpile of ivory, and some is harvested legally). When you have a rehair done the bow maker will closely examine the tip for any hairline cracks around. If there are any, the tip must be replaced immediately.

Top See *belly.*

Tuner The metal implement that is attached to the tailpiece and holds the lower end of the string, allowing for fine-tuning without using the pegs. A great source of buzzing, especially on cellos.

Undercoat See *ground.*

Underslide The plate, usually of highly figured abalone or mother of pearl, on the underside of the frog. It slides out to reveal the mortise where the lower plug holds the hair in place. Fragile, and easily corroded by perspiration, it occasionally has to be replaced.

Varnish The coating that protects the wood, gives the instrument much of its beauty, and affects the sound. The lore surrounding violin varnish is rich; its precise makeup and effect on an instrument are the "big mystery." In truth, everybody uses pretty much the same thing: resins and a drying oil dissolved in turpentine. But every maker jealously guards his or her own recipe, which is usually the result of years of experimentation. Violin varnish has to be made rather than purchased off the shelf, because what works acoustically is, in the world of commercial varnish, an abject failure. Any surface coating has a dampening effect on vibration, and modern varnishes are simply too durable. It doesn't always correlate, but usually the better the violin, the more fragile the varnish that was used on it. Aesthetically, a great varnish has a depth and texture that enhances the character of the wood without obscuring or staining it. See *ground*.

Volute On the scroll, the spiral that sits atop the pegbox.

Wedge The small piece of wood between the tongue of the frog and the hank of hair that spreads the hair flat. If the hair is bunching up, the wedge needs replacing.

Winding 1. The alloys wrapped around the cores of the instrument's strings. 2. See *lapping*.

Wrapping See *lapping*.

For information on violins, bows, insurance brokers, instrument retailers, repair shops, and suppliers, visit www.stringsmagazine.com for the easy-to-use Web version of the annual *Strings* magazine *Resource Guide*, which is accessible for free. See also *Strings* magazine (PO Box 767, San Anselmo, CA 94979; 4155-485-6946). An additional source of information for the British reader is the *British and International Music Yearbook* (Rhinegold Publishing, London).

For additional information on humidity and its effects on wood and your instrument, see the following:

Understanding Wood: a Craftsman's Guide to Wood Technology, by R. Bruce Hoadley (Taunton Press, Newton, Connecticut)

The Woodworker's Bible, by Alf Martensson (A & C Black Publishers, London)

Woodcarving: Tools, Materials and Equipment, by Chris Pye (Guild of Master Craftsmen Publications, Lewes, East Sussex)

Visit www.fpl.fs.fed.us/ to gain on-line access to the *Wood Handbook: Wood as an Engineering Material* (Forest Products Society, Madison, Wisconsin).

CONTRIBUTORS

Susan M. Barbieri is a writer and editor in St. Paul, Minnesota, who contributes to *Minnesota Monthly* magazine and to "Sounding Board," the monthly newsletter of the American Composers Forum. She has been playing the violin for four years.

Peg Baumgartel is a bow maker and restorer and a member of the American Federation of Violin and Bow Makers and the Violin Society of America. She has been awarded numerous certificates from international bow-making competitions, and she drew the technical illustrations in Christopher Brown's *Double Bass Bow* book. She apprenticed with Paul Siefried in Los Angeles and is a veteran of the Oberlin Bowmaking Workshop.

David Burgess makes and repairs violins, violas, and cellos and has won numerous international awards for his instruments. He has served as a judge in instrument-making competitions, and several of his instruments are part of permanent collections at the Smithsonian Museum. His writing has appeared in the *Wall Street Journal, Strings, Strad,* and other newspapers and TV and radio broadcasts.

Yung Chin is a bow maker and dealer of bows based in New York City. He is also the current director of the Oberlin Bowmaking Workshop and a frequent contributor to *Strings* magazine.

Julie Lyonn Lieberman is an improvising violinist, singer, composer, educator, recording artist, author, and producer. The author of five books, including *You Are Your Instrument* and *The Contemporary Violinist,* she has also written and coproduced seven programs for National Public Radio on jazz violin. Formerly on the faculty at Juilliard, she is now a professor with The New School's Jazz and Contemporary Music Department.

Strings' contributing Editor **Jana Luckey** is associate principal cello of the Toledo Symphony and makes frequent appearances in recital and as a soloist in Ohio and southeast Michigan. She holds a master's degree in performance from the Cleveland Institute of Music and a bachelor's in psychology from Bryn Mawr College.

James N. McKean is a violin maker in New York City. A corresponding editor for *Strings* and the author of *Commonsense Instrument Care*, he is also a past president of the American Federation of Violin and Bow Makers.

Wendy Moes makes violins, violas, and cellos with Peter Moes in Stamford, Connecticut. They also specialize in sales, sound adjustments, repairs, and restorations of fine old instruments.

Stacy Phillips is the author of 17 books on various aspects of fiddling, including the forthcoming *Fiddle Tunes for Viola and Cello* and *Fiddle Tunes for Two Violas,* both published by Mel Bay. His slide guitar work is featured on Eileen Ivers' album *Crossing the Bridge,* on Sony Classical.

Jessamyn Reeves-Brown is the former editor of *Strings* magazine. She attended Vassar College, where she played in the orchestra and sang in the madrigal choir. She also has played guitar and sung folk-rock with her multi-instrumentalist husband under the name of Songsmyth. When not making music or massaging words, she creates historical costumes; *Jessamyn's Regency Costume Companion* can be found at www.songsmyth.com.

The late **Mark R. Reindorf** was a violinist and dealer in rare bows. He worked in the shop of Jacques Français in New York and later moved to San Francisco. He was a student of Ivan Galamian and Dorothy DeLay. His article on the condition of bows first ran in *Strings'* Fall 1988 issue.

Strings' Associate Editor **Heather K. Scott,** a writer, editor, and photographer living in the San Francisco Bay Area, grew up playing viola and piano. She has covered music and the arts for such publications as the *Santa Barbara Independent,* Citysearch.com, and *Piano & Keyboard* magazine.

Richard Ward has been associated with Ifshin Violins in Berkeley, California, for over ten years. He began playing the violin at age ten and has been a violinist with several Bay Area orchestas, including the Vallejo Symphony Orchestra for the last 13 years. He holds a master's degree in fine arts and photography from Indiana University.

INDEX

Bold numbers indicate pages with photographs.